LORD MAYORS OF LONDON

by Anna Milford

Drawings by Sue Stafford

Illustrations based on old prints, paintings and documents.

Picture research AnnaConda

One of the London Pride Collection

Comerford and Miller

36 Grosvenor Road, West Wickham, Kent BR4 9PY

To SIMON
Trooper in the Honourable Artillery Company who marched in the Lord Mayor's
Show, 12 November 1988

By the same Author:
Ring the Bells of London Town
Slay us a Dragon

Acknowledgements
Alderman Sir Alan Traill; Alderman Brian Jenkins; James Sewell, Archivist, and
Juliet Bankes, Deputy Archivist, Corporation of London Records Office; Lee Waite,
Senior City Guides Lecturer; Rosalind Hutchinson, Guild of Guide Lecturers; Sue
Stafford, Merchant Taylor; John Copeman, Baker; Tony Davies, Vintner; Vivian
Ilchester, Air Pilot and Navigator; Robin Wilson, Pavior; John Young, Solicitor; John
Yule, Clothworker; Bunny Morgan, City Livery Club; Peter Matthews, London
Tourist Board; Alfred Goldstein; David Ballard; Guildhall Library; Museum of
London; London Library; Tonbridge School; Christ's Hospital; City of London
School; Westerham Library; Oxted Library; Whitbread Brewery; Ring & Brymer;
Trusthouse Forte; City Guides Course colleagues: Woody Woodnutt, John
Normandale, Lionel Roberts, 'City Recorder'; 'City Post'.
Printed in Great Britain by View Publications, Bristol

© Anna Milford 1989

ISBN 1 871204 06 2

Front cover illustration: WILLIAM WALWORTH - the Mayor who killed Wat Tyler.

CONTENTS

The Mayoralty

Miscellany of Mayors

Indicies

FOREWORD

Anna Milford has achieved the impossible. Having written a full-sized text on the history of The Lord Mayor of London, by careful editing she has reduced it down to a reference and pocket-sized publication.

In doing so it loses none of its authenticity and readability. On the contrary she has very carefully researched the history and explains why the unique structure of government of "The Square Mile" can still work today, serving both The City and our Country. I certainly learned a lot from reading it.

Above all else she has satisfied a great need by producing such a book which I am sure will gain a wide distribution. I have lost count of the number of times when I have been asked for a publication on The Mayoralty. Genuine interest has grown particularly during this year, 1989, when we are celebrating the 800th Anniversary of The Lord Mayor of London.

Those of us who value the traditions and heritage of our City, handed down over the centuries, are in Anna Milford's debt. We wish this book every success.

Sir Alan Traill G.B.E., M.A., D.Mus.
Lord Mayor of London 1984/1985

London's First Citizen

The Lord Mayor

'THE Lord Mayor, with all his medieval array and his medieval officers, is to me a Historic Monument which ought never to be removed'.

A century after Walter Besant wrote that plea the historic monument is still in place, but who is the Lord Mayor of London and what does he do?

Seven million people live in Greater London, but the Lord Mayor of London is overlord of only the Square Mile, home to less than 10,000 of them. All the other boroughs have their own Mayors and Councils, Westminster even has its own Lord Mayor, but the man in the Mansion House is always premier Mayor in the capital, and the nation.

Not until Henry VIII did the title *Lord* Mayor come into common usage, and on certain historic occasions he is still referred to as plain 'Mayor'.

The first Mayor, Henry Fitzailwyn, is mentioned in the reign of Richard the Lionheart, and the 800th anniversary of his appointment fell in 1989, the year of office of Christopher Collett.

In the Middle Ages a Mayor sometimes served several years in succession, and many were elected two or three times. On occasion the King dismissed or imprisoned the Mayor, and in one lethal year three Mayors in succession were carried off by the sweating Sickness.

The City of London has always jealously guarded its independence and has frequently been at odds with the court and the Parliament at Westminster. There has never been an Earl of London, nor was any Royal favourite ever foisted on the City as its leader, and Londoners have always chosen one of their own for First Citizen.

Late medieval London clustered within the Roman wall, and what was already becoming known as the 'Cittie' was separated from the Royal Palace, the Parliament and the Abbey at Westminster by open fields and the village of Charing. Today the boundaries of the 'City' or the 'Square Mile' are guarded by the heraldic dragons of the Corporation of London, and defined by its bye-laws.

The modern Lord Mayor wears many hats, besides the befeathered tricorne he waves out of his coach at the Lord Mayor's Show.

He is Chairman of the Court of Aldermen and the Court of Common Council. Chief Magistrate of the City and tenant of the Mansion House, which boasts the only justice court in a private residence. Trustee of St Paul's, Chancellor of the City University, Governor of the Royal Hospital and Coroner of London.

He is piped aboard any warship in the Thames as Admiral of the Port of London, and is Commander of the City Forces. Only three army regiments and the Royal Marines and the Honourable Artillery Company have the historic right to march through the City 'drums beating, colours flying and bayonets fixed'. On state occasions the HAC can fire 21-gun salutes from the Tower without asking his permission.

He has the right of audience to the Sovereign and the rank of an Earl during his year of office. He announces the death of a monarch, and after proclaiming the new one carries the Crystal Sceptre in the coronation procession.

He is entitled to any sturgeon caught below London Bridge, to drive sheep over it and to any cattle that fall off it. Finally, he is entrusted under the Monarch's Sign with the password to the Tower.

After greeting the Queen at Temple Bar with the Sword and Keys of the City he is then responsible for her safety, and will sit on her right at table, above the heir to the throne – a privilege granted by Henry V.

On goodwill visits abroad he enjoys a unique role as a non-political national figure on the international stage, and at home entertains distinguished visitors on behalf of the Sovereign and the government. The Prime Minister makes a major policy statement at his first Guildhall Banquet, and at one of his last Mansion House dinners the Chancellor of the Exchequer and the Governor of the Bank of England both make important financial speeches.

The rents, rates and business turnover of the City are greater than the total revenue of many a sovereign nation, and the only comparable state whose size is in inverse ratio to its influence is the Vatican. One of the few things the Lord Mayor cannot do, unlike the master of the *Citta del Vaticano*, is run his own diplomatic corps and issue his own stamps. The Square Mile is a global money market, well placed by the clock between Tokyo and New York. Beside the Bank of England, the Stock Exchange and Lloyds are the Baltic Exchange for ship and air broking, the petroleum, metal and commodity Exchanges, Lloyds Register for the worldwide classification of Shipping and hundreds of international banks and finance houses.

Britain is no longer the 'workshop of the world', but these 'invisible earnings' of the City help to keep the country's balance of payments out of the red, while the odd black sheep among the gizmo dealers and widget brokers are rounded up by the 70 strong Fraud Squad of the City Police.

To be head of the City Corporate and the City Financial calls for ability, integrity, diplomacy and above all stamina. A Lord Mayor of the mid-1970s calculated he had listened to 5000 speeches, made around 800 and attended over 300 banquets, and the current schedule is even more formidable. There are also national, and several international, visits and in addition participation at innumerable receptions, luncheons, award-givings, tree-plantings, chambers of commerce, pensioners' parties, financial seminars, children's plays, concerts, exhibitions and lectures which will involve the shaking of well over 50,000 hands.

Election to Lord Mayor is no longer the last step in a distinguished career, but one taken well before retirement beckons, and it stems from the law reforms that compelled magistrates, and therefore aldermen, to step down from the bench at the age of 70. To progress through Freeman, Alderman, Sheriff and finally Lord Mayor and still have at least a dozen useful years service to the Corporation after having 'passed the chair' it has become necessary to start up the civic ladder much earlier. The ruling, first seen as a heavy blow, has in reality proved a bonus with people in their forties and fifties now filling the highest positions, and a few years back the Mansion House even echoed to the laughter of tiny Mayoral siblings.

Nor are present Lord Mayors expected to be 'gentlemen with deep pockets', eager to entertain at their own expense for a twelvemonth before donating a costly addition to the Gold Plate Collection in the Vaults as a final gesture.

The Mayoral year finally ends on the second Friday in November, the day of the Ceremony of Silent Change, when he and his wife take tea with their successors. They then pack their bags and slip out of the side door of the Mansion House to vanish from the civic scene until the following Easter Monday.

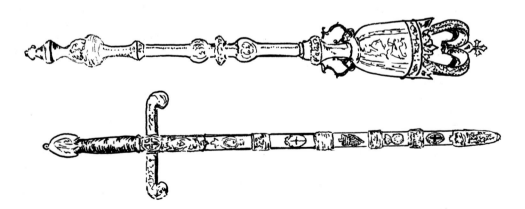

The Lord Mayor mace and State sword

'To Choose Every Year a Mayor'

The Election

MICHAELMAS DAY, 29th September, is the last hurdle for any aspiring Lord Mayor. Prior to this, a candidate must have stood for selection on three previous occasions — as a Freeman, as an Alderman and as Sheriff. Four, if he was previously a Common Councilman, so the timespan is at least ten or fifteen years.

Unless death, disaster or scandal intervene the name of the next Lord Mayor-Elect is the most open secret in the City, and he is not expected to be overcome with amazement when the Liverymen's choice falls on him in Guildhall. His colleagues among the chartered accountants, solicitors, bankers or businessmen will be well prepared to deputise for him in the office, while his future diaries will have filled up with a daunting list of civic engagements long before his predecessor quits the Chair.

Election Day starts with a service in St Lawrence Jewry and while the Corporation dignitaries, officials and the Masters of the Companies and their ladies are in church, Guildhall has been filling up. All 22,000 liverymen are entitled to vote, and about a thousand usually pass through the wooden wickets into Guildhall to do so.

After the Lord Mayor, Aldermen, Sheriffs and Officers are seated the Common Cryer commands 'all those not Liverymen to depart the Hall on pain of imprisonment'. Despite this dire warning the few members of the public present do not scurry out, so the times, if not the words, have changed.

'Oyez! Oyez! Oyez!' The good members of the Livery are reminded that they have come 'for the election of a fit and able person to be Lord Mayor of this City for the year ensuing. Draw near and give your attendance. God save the Queen'.

To show that no influence is being brought to bear the Lord Mayor, the Aldermen who have 'passed the chair', the Town Clerk, Recorder, City Marshal and Swordbearer retire to the Livery Hall and the election then proceeds.

The names of four persons who have served as Sheriff are read out by the Common Serjeant. He then repeats them individually in the traditional manner, and the expected responses are given:

'So many of you as will have Alfred W .... all'.
'So many of you as will have Hubert X .... next year'.
'So many of you as will have Simon Y .... later'.
'So many of you as will have Paul Z .... later'.

He then announces, to laughter, 'in view of that display of solidarity your choice has fallen on Alfred W.. and Hubert X..' and then goes off to inform the Aldermen.

While they deliberate between this pair a short lecture is given on some historical aspect of the City, and then doors are thrown open and the Aldermen reappear. Cheers break out when it is seen that Alfred W.. is walking on the left of the Lord Mayor. The Town Clerk calls upon him as Lord Mayor-Elect to declare his assent, and then places round his neck the collar he had worn two or three years previously as Sheriff, before the Common Cryer winds up the proceedings:

'Oyez! Oyez! Oyez! You good members of the Livery ..... may depart hence at this time, and give your attendance here again upon a new summons. God save the Queen'.

A month later the Lord Mayor-Elect goes to the House of Lords to hear from the Lord Chancellor the Sovereign's approval of the citizens choice. On the second Friday in November he takes office at the Ceremony of Silent Change. At this short and simple ceremony the only words spoken are those of the Oath, administered by the Town Clerk and repeated by the new Lord Mayor-Elect. Taking the seat of the outgoing Lord Mayor he accepts in silence, the Sceptre, the Seal, the City's Purse, the Sword and the Mace.

Thousands of Londoners line the streets next day when the new Lord Mayor 'shows' himself to the people, but his legal duty is to sign a declaration before Her Majesty's judges at the Law Courts in the Strand. This sheet of velum depicts the royal arms, the City arms and the arms of the new Lord Mayor and his livery Company, and the Declaration is written in fine copper-plate with a quill pen. It is as exquisite as any illuminated manuscript in the Archives, and a masterpiece of the Painter-Stainer's art.

The Declaration is simple: 'I, ..., do solemnly, sincerely and truly declare that I will faithfully perform the duties of my office as Lord Mayor of the City of London'. Thereafter he uses only his surname as an official signature, 'Whittington – Mayor'.

His wife bears the courtesy title of the Lady Mayoress, but the lady elected First Citizen in 1983 was always correctly referred to as the *Lord* Mayor.

Left, Mercers.
Right, Merchant Taylors

The first three mayors were all Mercers

Attendant on the Mayor

Ceremonial Officers

THE Common Clerk, took his duties seriously and compiled in the early 15th century the 'Liber Albus', the White Book, as a guide for his successors as Town Clerk. Its procedures are still followed with little alteration today,but the Mayor's ceremonial officers have now been pruned down to a paltry three.

THE SWORD BEARER is unmistakable in an immense fur hat (busby) of Russian sable, successor to the 'goodly royale hatt' given by Mayor Bowes in 1546. Its wearer was once a military officer so he remains covered on all occasions, indoors and out, civic and royal. A curious object is carved above the stone crest on Guildhall porch, to some it is a granite sponge or petrified brain coral, but to others it is clearly the Sword Bearer's goodly hat.

THE COMMON CRYER, Sergeant-at-Arms and Mace Bearer are one and the same individual, and though a new monarch is 'proclaimed' on the steps of the Royal Exchange by the Lord Mayor, it is the Common Cryer who reads the document. Edward III granted the right to the Mayor to have a Mace carried before him, and many Companies have their maces carried by beadles at Common Hall. The Sergeant Cryer was provided with a horse, 'for the honour of the City' and twelve pence for every official 'Cry'.

THE CITY MARSHAL wears a resplendent uniform and plumed helmet, and has more often been a soldier than a sailor since good horsemanship is essential. Originally he headed the Watch and Ward in the City, rounded up rogues and vagabonds and had lepers ejected outside the walls. He rides, or walks, ahead of the Lord Mayor in all processions to clear the way, and also 'marshals' ceremonial events with the help of a less splendidly attired staff.

Other picturesque personages from the 'Liber Albus' have disappeared into the 'dark, backward and abysm of time', but the individual known as the Common Hunt survived almost into living memory.

Royal forests were closely guarded and the game laws draconian — Australia is full of families whose ancestors were transported for poaching pheasants or snaring rabbits. It was therefore a notable privilege when Henry I granted the 'Council' the rights of the chase in Surrey, Middlesex and the Chiltern Hills.

The Mayor kept his own pack of hounds, and the Common Hunt in his cap and breeches was in attendance at Mansion House banquets and lived in premises off the City Road, complete with kennels and vast boilers for stewing meat to feed his pack.

Sergeant-at-Arms

The Sword Bearer

The Mayor and Mayoress in their finery

The Wardrobe

THE Lady Mayoress will need scores of suits, dresses, evening gowns and hats to see her through the year, but the Lord Mayor too boasts a wardrobe of which any monarch would be proud.

At most daytime functions, be it a bankers' lunch an opening or a tree planting, he wears a morning suit. Black coat and striped trousers, with the Mayoral badge on a ribbon.

As chairman of the Court of Alderman and of the Court of Common Council there will be a furred gown over the morning suit, but on major civic occasions he wears the scarlet robe of an alderman with a starched lace jabot.

For banquets or state visits at Guildhall or the Mansion House the Black and Gold Entertaining Gown makes its appearance. It is of stiff silk and so weighted with gold thread that it could be mistaken for the robe of a Lord Chancellor or the Rector of a university. Beneath is traditional court dress of black knee breeches, silk stockings and buckled shoes.

For a Royal occasion such as the wedding of the Prince of Wales at St Paul's, the Queen was received in the crimson velvet and ermine robes of an earl.

The tricorne hat, so in evidence on the day of the Lord Mayor's Show, is the only official headgear and the ostrich feathers take quite a battering when waved out of alternate windows of the coach all one November day. Formality in dress and behaviour is also expected of the Lord Mayor's guests. A stiff directive was issued from the Mansion House in 1980 after the 'latitude' permitted in matters of evening attire had long been extended too far. Wearers of Dinner Jackets embellished with 'velvet ties of varying hues, coloured shirts and shirts with frills, cummerbunds and the like' had been noted.

Although accepting that not all younger Liverymen could afford white tie and tails, only those so attired were acceptable at the top table. Gentlemen in Dinner Jackets would be tolerated below the salt, 'provided that this means a *black tie and white shirt* without garish modern accompaniments'.

THE INSIGNIA. The gold Collar of double 'SS' was bequeathed to the mayoralty by John Allen in 1545, and from it is suspended a jewelled Badge. The present one was made in 1802 and later reset. It consists of 24 rose cut diamonds around a cameo decorated with roses, thistles and shamrocks. It is surrounded by a garter and bears the City arms, St George's cross with the sword of St Paul, and the motto *'Domine dirige Nos'* – God direct us. A Victorian wreath was added to enclose the garter in 1880.

The Collar and Badge together are worn on formal occasions, but for everyday the Badge alone suspended from a dark blue ribbon.

The Great Mace has been carried in front of the Lord Mayor since 1354, and rests on the table during meetings of the Court of Common Council. The original was stolen under the Commonwealth, and the Restoration Mace presented by Lord Mayor Vyner lasted less than a hundred years. The present massive one in silver gilt dates from George II, and is no trifling bauble. It weighs in at 20lbs and is topped by a crown decorated with fleur-de-lis.

It is the privilege of the Lord Mayor to carry the Crystal Sceptre at a coronation, relic of the days when he assisted the hereditary Chief Butler. The jewelled gold head is 15th century, but part of the shaft is thought to be Saxon.

16th Century Lord Mayor and his Lady

The City Purse, a drawstring bag embroidered with the City arms and a gift of Queen Elizabeth contains, the Common Seal. The Seal is carried to Westminster when the Lord Mayor Elect is presented to the Lord Chancellor.

The obverse of the Seal shows St Paul, as it has always done, holding his sword and the arms of England. In the early 13th century a new Seal was made with London's very own saint on the reverse, Thomas Becket, and the words *me que te peperi ne cesses Thomas tueri* — 'cease not, Thomas, to guard me who brought you forth'. At the Reformation this was destroyed as superstitious and a new reverse designed with the City arms and the words *Londini defende tuos Deus optime cives* — 'most Gracious God defend thy Citizens of London'. Official documents are stamped with the imprint of this Seal in wax.

The heraldic blazon of the City arms is 'argent (silver), a cross gules (red) in the first quarter a sword in pale point upwards of the first. On either side a dragon with wings elevated and endorsed argent and charged on the wing with a cross gules.

There is a whole armoury of swords, the most precious being the Pearl Sword and Scabbard presented by Elizabeth I. This is the one proffered by Lord Mayor when the monarch enters the City at Temple Bar. It is touched by the royal hand in acknowledgement and then returned to its keeper.

In most of the City churches there is a sword rest in front of the Lord Mayor's pew in which the sword is placed upright during the service. Many of these wrought iron rests enclose the shields of Lord Mayor's connected with the parish, but in St Helen's Bishopsgate, associated with Lord Mayors Andrew Judde and John Lawrence, the sword rest is of wood.

The Black Sword is intended for the solemn days of Lent and in times of official mourning. When the Lord Mayor sits at the Central Criminal Court as the 'Chief Commissioner of Assize', the Old Bailey Sword is always behind his seat which is in the centre of the bench of judges.

Two embroidered Seal bags 1319

I William the King

London's Charters

AFTER the Battle of Hastings William of Normandy chose negotiation rather than a prolonged and bloody siege to gain the capital. For that reason he is never 'William the Conqueror' in the City. Terms were agreed and he was crowned in Westminster Abbey on Christmas Day 1066. The following year he granted a Charter to London, but to show who was master of the realm he drew up plans to build the White Tower on its eastern boundary.

The Charter is a slip of parchment measuring no more than six inches by two, with the remains of William's seal attached. It is kept deep in the Archives of Guildhall, and is very occasionally put on show. It is a truly remarkable document, not least for having survived intact since 1067, and for its brevity and for being written in Anglo- Saxon, not Norman French. It states:

'I William the King, greet William the Bishop and Godfrey the Portreeve, and all the Burgesses within London, French and English friendly. And I acquaint you, that I will that ye be all the laws worthy that were in King Edward's day. And I will that every child be his father's heir, after his father's day. And I will not suffer that any man to do you any wrong. God preserve you.'

Having read that it is possible to understand the original:

'Will'm kyng gret Will'm, bisceop and Gosfreg portirefan, and ealle thea burhwaru binnan Londone, Frencisce and Englisce freonflice. and ic kyde eow that ic wylle that gey boen eallra thoera laga weorde the gy waeran on Eadwerdes daege kynges. and ic wylle that aelc cylk beo his faeder yrfnume. aefter his faederdaege. and ic nelle getholian thaet aenig man eow aenig wrang beode. God eow gehealde'.

Richard I, in return for cash to go crusading, gave the citizens the right to appoint a mayor, and a goldsmith Henry Fitzailwyn was their first choice. When the money ran out the King bartered his crown and the bed of the Thames for more, and from this stems the Mayor's title of Admiral of the Port of London.

Richard was treacherously imprisoned by the Austrian emperor, and the Londoners had to fork out more money towards the ransom. The Emperor Leopold used this ill-gotten windfall to rebuild the walls of Vienna which were only demolished when the *Ringstrasse* was constructed in the 19th century.

The Mayor, Serlo le Mercer, was ranked among the lords at Runnymede for the sealing of Magna Carta in 1215. In an earlier charter that year King John conceded 'that the City shall have its ancient liberties and free customs, both by land and water ... and to choose *every* year a mayor and present him to us'. This marked the beginning of the annual elections of a Mayor, although John's actions were motivated not by love of the London merchants, but his vengeful urge to weaken the power of the bishops and the barons.

The City was, and still is, a municipality with no charter of incorporation, and the unique 'Custom of London' and its ancient liberties are recognised as dating back earlier than 1189. This provides an irrefutable answer to every quibble since it refers to a legal cut-off date, 'beyond which the memory of man runs not to the contrary'.

It was not all in a day's work for the chosen citizen to call on the king, for if he was away on a Royal Progress around the country it meant trailing after him for weeks to gain the royal approval to take office. Nor was it an empty ceremony when he got there, for Henry III vetoed nine Mayors in his long reign, and jailed another who died in prison.

But with their wealth and power the Mayor and Commonalty could usually outmanoeuvre the monarch, as to their cost Richard II, Charles I and James II were to learn too late.

The annoyance of playing 'hunt the king' was finally eliminated when the Chief Justice in Westminster Hall took over the role on behalf of the sovereign. It is now the Lord Chancellor, down the road in the House of Lords, who conveys the Sovereign's approval to the Lord Mayor Elect in October.

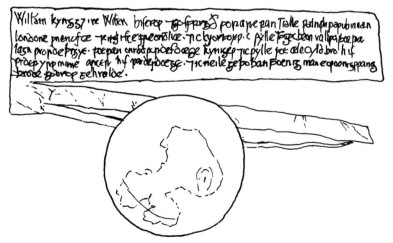

London's Charter, with the remains of William I seal.

The Great Ceremonial Parade

The Lord Mayor's Show

THE ceremonial parade of the new Mayor has been known as the Riding, the Pageante, the Procession and finally the Show. It had peaks and troughs of popularity and even Pepys, who seldom missed it, did admit one year that 'the pageants which were many, were in themselves but poor and absurd'.

But twelve months later that disappointment was forgotten in the sight of the Thames awash with a positively Venetian flotilla of Company craft. The Lord Mayor's barge was 'accosted by a vessel bearing Galatea in a seahorse chariot drawn by dolphins ridden by sirens playing on harps; sealions too, ridden by Tritons with Pipes and Hornes antique'.

By 1841 the ships had taken to the streets as 'floats', and a fully rigged and manned East Indiaman was the centre piece of John Pirie's Show. But attitudes were changing, and there were many powerful critics who ridiculed these antiquated exhibitions as symptomatic of the deeper malaise underlying the Corporation.

The 'Times' led the sarcastic chorus, but the Show weathered the storm and continued to fill the November streets with galleons, castles, giants, dragons, nymphs and shepherds, and anything else that caught the mood of the moment.

Topicality was all the rage, but in 1879 the Commander-in-Chief meanly refused permission for '50 survivors of the detachment engaged at Rorke's Drift to attend the Procession'. That epic stand of Redcoats against the *impis* of Cetawayo was re-enacted in the film 'Zulu', but to Londoners of Francis Truscott's Day it would have been the only chance to cheer some of the eleven Victoria Cross holders.

In 1883 a heroine's name was on every lip, Grace Darling, and the frail wooden boat in which she and her father had rowed out to save the men of the 'Forfarshire' was in Robert Fowler's Show. Another boat was in George Nottage's Show next year. The Sudan Campaign was at its height, and this was a replica of the *felucca* used by Lord Wolseley on the Nile. Old Sir Garnet after losing an eye in the Crimea had gone on to fight in Burma, the Indian Mutiny, Chinese and Canadian revolts and then taken command in Africa. He was the one to present the VCs in the field to the men of Rorke's Drift.

By 1889 efforts to improve relations with France were bearing fruit, and Henry Isaacs did his bit by inviting the 'Sapeurs Pompiers de France et d'Algerie' to join his Show. Tactfully English firemen from 29 brigades were

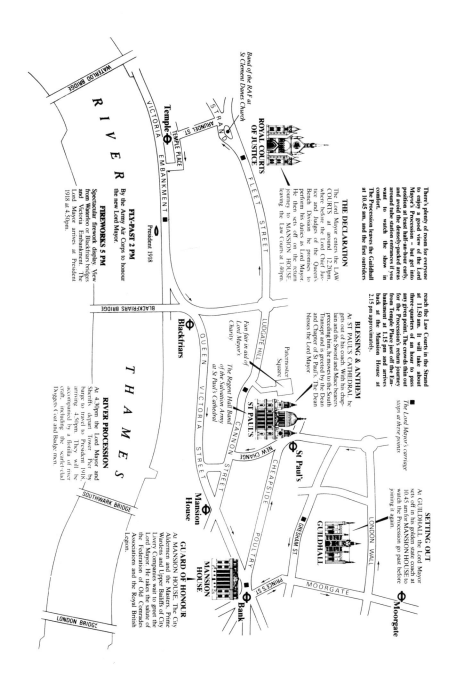

WATERLOO BRIDGE

R I V E R

VICTORIA EMBANKMENT

Temple · **TEMPLE PLACE**

STRAND · **ARUNDEL ST**

Band of the RAF at St Clement Danes Church

ROYAL COURTS OF JUSTICE

FLEET STREET

There's plenty of room for everyone to enjoy a good view of the Lord Mayor's Procession - but get into position at least half-an-hour early, and avoid the densely-packed areas around tube station entrances if you want to watch the show in comfort.
The Procession leaves the Guildhall at 10.45 am, and the first outriders

THE DECLARATION
The Lord Mayor enters the LAW COURTS at around 12.20pm, where before the Lord Chief Justice and Judges of the Queen's Bench Division he promises to perform his duties as Lord Mayor. He then sets off on the return journey to MANSION HOUSE, leaving the Law Courts at 1.44pm.

FLY-PAST 2 PM
By the Army Air Corps to honour the new Lord Mayor.

President 1918

FIREWORKS 5 PM
Spectacular firework display. View from Waterloo or Blackfriars bridges and Victoria Embankment. The Lord Mayor arrives at President 1918 at 4.50pm.

BLACKFRIARS BRIDGE

Blackfriars

reach the Law Courts in the Strand at 11.50 am. It will take about three-quarters of an hour to pass any given point. The crowds thin out for the Procession's return journey from Temple Place just off the Embankment at 1.15 pm and arrives back at the Mansion House at 2.15 pm approximately.

BLESSING & ANTHEM
At ST PAUL'S CATHEDRAL he gets out of his coach. With his chaplain and the Sword and Mace bearers preceding him, he moves to the South Transept and is greeted by the Dean and Chapter of St Paul's. The Dean blesses the Lord Mayor

SETTING OUT
At GUILDHALL, the Lord Mayor sets off in his golden state coach at 10.45 am for MANSION HOUSE to watch the Procession go past before joining it again.

The Lord Mayor's carriage stops at these points

LUDGATE HILL

Paternoster Square

Fun fair in aid of Lord Mayor's Charity

The Regent Hall Band of the Salvation Army at St Paul's Cathedral

ST PAUL'S · **St Paul's**

QUEEN VICTORIA STREET

NEW CHANGE

CANNON STREET

CHEAPSIDE

Mansion House

POULTRY

GRESHAM ST

GUILDHALL

LONDON WALL

Moorgate · **MOORGATE**

PRINCE ST

MANSION HOUSE

Bank

T H A M E S

SOUTHWARK BRIDGE

LONDON BRIDGE

RIVER PROCESSION
At 4.30pm the Lord Mayor and Sheriffs depart Tower Pier by barge to travel to President 1918, arriving 4.50pm. They will be accompanied by a flotilla of river craft, including the scarlet-clad Doggett's Coat and Badge men.

GUARD OF HONOUR
At MANSION HOUSE. The City Aldermen and the Masters, Prime Wardens and Upper Bailiffs of City Livery Companies wait to greet the Lord Mayor. He takes the salute of the Federation of Old Comrades Associations and the Royal British Legion.

placed ahead of these foreigners to maintain good relations within the 'Entente Cordiale'.

David Evans in 1891 was a Welshman and took the Principality for his theme. Girls in steeple hats surrounded Edward I and the first Prince of Wales, and peering out of the leeks and daffodils were droves of harpists, bards and druids and floats of the Welsh industries of Iron, Coal, Tin and Slate.

The nearest thing to a display of armed might was George Faudel- Phillips' Show of 1896, dedicated to the 'History of Uniforms'. The final float was a solitary Maxim gun mounted on a horse-drawn carriage − preceded by a motor car, but not a man with a red flag.

William Treloar's Show of 1906 was a historic pageant of mayors, one for each century: Henry Fitzailwyn for the 13th, John Philpot the 14th, Richard Whittington the 15th, Richard Gresham the 16th, Thomas Myddyleton the 17th, John Wilkes the 18th and Robert Waithman the 19th. A contemporary touch came from aged veterans of the five regiments which took part in the Charge of the Light Brigade.

But by 1915 young soldiers filled the streets, and Charles Wakefield's Day was known as the 'Recruiting Show'. Captured enemy guns featured in the parade, and the loudest cheers rang out for men of the new Royal Flying Corps and Anti-Aircraft Corps.

The Show revived after each world war but complaints grew over the traffic congestion when Lord Mayor's Day fell on a weekday. In 1950 the Corporation retaliated to the attacks being co-ordinated by the Daily Express and Evening Standard, and then suggested a compromise. Why not 'confine the Show to a small dignified Procession with a small escort of cavalry which would not interfere with traffic at all'?

This paltry offer was treated with contempt by the united opposition who had no wish to have their gigantic street party curtailed, and the argument raged on. Finally, in 1959, the Show was quietly altered to the 'Saturday after the second Friday in November'.

Every Show still has its theme: in 1988 Christopher Collett chose 'People Count'; Greville Spratt encouraged everyone in 1987 to 'Make an Effort for Britain'; in 1986 David Rowe-Ham selected 'Capital City; Allan Davies brightened 1985 by 'Service with a Smile' and in 1984 Alan Traill as a musician believed in 'Living with Harmony'.

The Lord Mayor's Coach was built in 1757 by Joseph Berry to a design of Sir Robert Taylor, and decorated with mythological panels by Cipriani. It weighs nearly three tons, and every alderman contributed £60 towards the total cost of £1065.

It has no springs, and until very recently it had no brakes, and it sways sickeningly on leather straps. A sailor Lord Mayor was heard to complain that he was 'never, never sick at sea, but he felt sick as a dog in that damned coach'. It is kept in the Museum of London on a floating platform to maintain humidity, and as a deterrent to vandals.

A month before the Show, shire horses traditionally supplied by Whitbread's Brewery begin practising with a dray laden with barrels to simulate the same weight, and the coach is taken to the Whitbread Stables a few days in advance so they can try out the real thing with their coachman.

John Lawless, in his magnificent scarlet and gold coat, white knee breeches and plumed hat, has driven the coach for twenty years, and also drove the Speaker's coach in the Queen's Silver Jubilee procession. That one is kept permanently at Whitbreads and only needs two horses, but he found it far more difficult to drive than his six horse team drawing the Lord Mayor's coach. The only thing he dreads on Show Day is rain.

Six horses are chosen from among the pairs who normally work the City streets — Time and Tide, Windsor and Washington, High and Mighty, Pikeman and Musketeer, or Pomp and Circumstance. Two youngsters are Tyson, a tough'un and Bowler, who bowls along. All stand over 18 hands tall, and it takes the farrier three hours to shoe just one.

There were 300 working horses in 1900, but these are now down to 32 delivering beer within a five mile radius of Whitbread's which has stood north of the Barbican since 1750. Each horse gets through 5lbs of carrots and 60lbs of fodder a day, and working in pairs they are still an economical way of pulling pints. No pollution, organically cost-effective and what traffic warden would dare stick a parking ticket on two tons of dapple grey horseflesh?

After the Lord Mayor's Show they are given an extra feed, Sunday as a day off and then back to work on Monday with their summer holidays to look forward to down on a Kentish hop farm — that is if they are not getting a bride to church on time, starring on television or 'moonlighting' in someone else's show.

The Procession of around 150 floats and bands is marshalled by the Pageant Master John Reid

The illustrated souvenir programmes are sold in aid of the new Lord Mayor's chosen charity, and Show Day ends with a bang of fireworks over the Thames by Blackfriars Bridge.

The Lord Mayor's Coach

Home for a year

The Mansion House

THE Lord Mayor must live in the private apartments of the Mansion House during his term of office, and only York, whose Mansion House was built earlier, still maintains a residence for its Lord Mayor.

Before it was built the Mayor lived in his own house and entertained at his livery hall, and it took years for the site to be agreed on the east bank of the Walbrook. Stocks Market and St Mary Woolnoth Haw Church were demolished, and Mayor Micajah Perry laid the foundation stone in 1739.

Handel was London's favourite composer at the time, and in 1752 George Dance's finished building was hailed as 'sedate, severe and dignified, a Hallelujah Chorus in stone'. After his Show, Mayor Crisp Gascoyne and Mrs Fanshaw moved in, but wagging tongues were disappointed when she proved to be the widower's daughter.

The main entrance facing the Bank of England has a pediment with a crowned London trampling on Envy, to the admiration of Plenty and Old Father Thames, but a modest doorway in Walbrook is now the usual access.

On the reception desk is a gilt telephone, the millionth instrument, presented by the Post Master General in 1938. There are extension numbers for the Swordbearer, Serjeant at Arms and Common Cryer, and the City Marshal, all three being the Lord Mayor's ceremonial officers. The Speech Researcher, the Yeoman and the Chef are also on call.

Dance had taken an optimistic view of the British weather and included an open atrium, but this was soon roofed over and became the Saloon. The original had also included an ungainly top storey, ridiculed as 'Noah's Ark and the Mare's Nest', which were removed shortly afterwards.

Among the treasures in the Saloon are four Windsor tapestries and two dozen gilt and crimson velvet Nile chairs. These were presented by the citizens to the Lord Mayor in 1797 after the battle and Nelson himself was guest of honour at the 1800 Show and Banquet. Two even larger gilt chairs are used by the Lord Mayor and Lady Mayoress at the Mansion House, but taken to Guildhall when Royalty is dining in state.

The Egyptian Hall is dominated by sixteen Corinthian columns with further columns above the cornice. The huge vault of the coved ceiling is decorated with stylised lotus flowers, the only truly Egyptian thing about the Hall. The Royal window overlooking Walbrook enshrines King John sulkily sealing Magna Carta, and Queen Elizabeth I sailing on the Thames. The City Window has a medley of William Walworth, Wat Tyler and the coronation of

Mansion House

Edward VI.

The two drawing rooms can be thrown together to make one, though the north one is always known as Wilkes Dining Parlour. The ballroom occupies the same space on the floor above, but is not included in any tour nor is the Lord Mayor's office in the Venetian Parlour.

A small hall and back stairs connect with the unique Justice Room, the only one in the world in a private house since Napoleon dispossessed the Doge of Venice.

Above the Lord Mayor's seat are the crossed emblems of Sword and Mace and the City Arms to show that he is in charge of Justic. A maximum of seven beaks can sit, but usually there are no more than two or three on the bench. Long-standing complaints that 'justice was not seen to be done' led to provision of a cramped public gallery in 1962

From inside the dock a hinged wooden lid lifts up to reveal a staircase down to the cells. Male prisoners are lodged separately but females have company, and at the height of the Suffragette campaign Emmeline Pankhurst was twice lodged in this 'birdcage'.

Offenders in the City south of a line from Leadenhall to Holborn Viaduct are tried at the Mansion House, felons north of this line are hauled up before the Mayor's Court at Guildhall.

Down in the Gold Vault behind a double door and protected by time locks are the treasures and Insignia of the City of London including the Pearl Sword, the Collar of Double 'SS' and the Fire Cup, the only item of civic plate salvaged in 1666.

The old Servants' Hall is now a cloakroom but the Rules of 1753 remain on the wall: 'Swear Not – Lie Not – Neither repeat old grievances. Whosoever eats or drinks in this Hall with his hat on shall forfeit sixpence or ride the wooden horse'.

Those fellows in furs

The Sheriffs

THE Mayor is a Johnny-come-lately compared to the Sheriffs. They have been appointed under Warrant of the Crown since before the time of Alfred the Great.

It took great wealth to be a Sheriff. Despite fines for refusing the honour, paying up still worked out far cheaper than a year dispensing hospitality to the citizens, and to ungrateful monarchs. It was a disgruntled George III who, seeing them dressed in their robes, carped at the Sheriffs as 'those fellows in furs'.

As royal officers the Port Reeve and the Shire Reeve dispensed justice in the King's name, and the people had to pay for the privilege in various ways. 'Sheriff-tooth' was an early form of land tenure where in lieu of rent, food and wine were supplied to the law court.

Sheriffs could be the poor man's friend against a grasping landlord, but no one willingly supports the Exchequer and it was their secondary role as tax collectors that made them so hated.

Richard the Lionheart was captured on his way back from the Third Crusade, and the Sheriff of Nottingham was carrying out his loyal task of raising the King's ransom when attacked by Robin Hood and his Merry Men in Sherwood Forest!

In 1381 Wat Tyler was provoked into killing one of the sheriff's men collecting the Poll Tax a contributory cause, along with the Black Death, of the Peasants Revolt.

Henry I confirmed the ancient liberties of London, but continued to appoint his own man as Port Reeve. His successor Stephen gave a 'sworn association of citizens' the right to choose the two sheriffs, for London and Middlesex, on condition that they met with his approval. A further step towards an independent London. Various Acts of Common Council followed in the 17th and 18th centuries opening the way for more general nominations, until in the 19th there were once over sixty candidates.

Nowadays expenditure and numbers of candidates have been curbed, and though the county has long lost its individual right, the Sheriffs are still 'of London and Middlesex'. One is customarily chosen from the ranks of the aldermen, and the other from the Livery. It is the Aldermanic Sheriff who is afterwards eligible and in line to be elected Lord Mayor.

On Midsummer Day, 24th June, the liverymen of the City of London are 'in Common Hall assembled', and if the election is contested the Lord Mayor, Recorder and aldermen who have 'passed the chair' retire to another room while they vote. The Sword is placed in front of them on a bed of roses, and since the rose symbolises silence anything said is confidential or *sub rosa*. They return for the announcement of the new Sheriffs-Elect, and as with the Lord Mayor-Elect those chosen seldom look totally surprised.

Two Bridgemasters are also elected, and four Aleconners at a salary of £10 a year. The aleconners once wore thick leather breeches when checking round the taverns, and if these breeches stuck to the seat on which a tankard had been spilled then they adjudged the ale 'as good as they were wont to brew'.

On 28th September the new Sheriffs are sworn in by the Town Clerk and then they then entertain their colleagues to the Sheriffs' Breakfast — actually lunch.

The shrieval chain is usually a gift from his electoral ward, livery company, colleagues and friends, and is his badge of office during the year, and a family heirloom thereafter. Fortunately he no longer has to find houseroom for a dozen emblazoned leather fire buckets, mementoes of the vain but valiant efforts of the sheriffs during the Great Fire.

The Lord Mayor, the Sheriffs and the Chief Commoner (leader of the Common Council) together with their spouses form the 'mayoral family'. They appear jointly or severally, and often perform as a harmonious octet when travelling to 'promote the City'.

Even so, though members of the Corporation, the Sheriffs are *not* part of the Lord Mayor's entourage nor can they deputise for him. In cases of illness or accident or having to be in two places at once, the Lord Mayor's place is usually taken by an alderman who has 'passed the chair'; an ex-Lord Mayor.

The role of the Sheriffs is to listen and learn, mastering the art and craft of the Mayoralty which may one day come their way. It is a year in the limelight, but when a Sheriff steps back into private life he has to live by the old City adage that 'there is nothing as dead as a ex-Sheriff'.

Not that their main functions take place in Guildhall at all but at *Old Bailey*, the Central Criminal Court.

Having long ago lost its own shrieval courts the Old Bailey is the City's main link with judiciary, and the Sheriffs have the right of audience to the Crown and to Parliament. The running costs come mainly from the City rates, although its judicial proceedings like all the other courts in the land are paid for by the Lord Chancellor's department and come under his authority.

The Lord Mayor is Chief Magistrate of the City and Old Bailey is its Crown Court, and it is as a Justice of the Peace in legal dress that he wears the Jewel on the great gold collar of double 'SS', on most other occasions it hangs from a ribbon. One of the reasons for the Court of Aldermen's right to veto elected candidates to their Court is to ensure that they are also suitable persons to automatically become magistrates.

One of the Sheriffs must be in attendance every day to 'bow in' Her Majesty's judges to their courts. When the Lord Mayor opens the new session, attended by his three ceremonial officers, he is greeted by the Sheriffs, the Secondary and the Under-Sheriff. The Sheriffs are responsible for the execution of writs and sentences, but the Under-Sheriff who actually carries out these legal duties. Criminal cases only are heard at Old Bailey and it is the court for Greater London and the Commonwealth as well as being used for sensational trials where jurors might be inhibited by local prejudice, as with the Yorkshire Ripper. It is also the court that hears cases of piracy and skullduggery on the high seas, and the more modern felony of aircraft hijacking. Hospitality to the judges is also the Sheriffs' responsibility, and much-coveted in the City is an invitation to lunch at Old Bailey.

The Magpie and Stump across the road hosted the judges and sheriffs until 1866, but few regret the passing of both the tavern and feast — those grisly 'hanging breakfasts' held in the shadow of the gallows outside Newgate. In 1864 one of the last public executions drew 50,000 spectators, and a prime view from the Magpie & Stump cost twenty guineas.

After eight centuries of infamy the jail was demolished and one of its iron gates is in the Museum of London, another was transported to Buffalo, USA. The Central Criminal Court was erected on the same site at the corner of Newgate Street and Old Bailey and opened by Edward VII in 1902.

The Recording Angel stands guard over the main porch above the inscription: 'Protect the children of the poor'. Over the Lord Mayor's entrance are the words: 'London shall have her ancient rights'

'Ye Good Men of the Livery'

The City Companies

LONDON'S first Mayor, Henry Fitzailwyn, was a goldsmith by trade and Company, and every Mayor since has belonged to one of the City Companies.

Craft and merchant guilds were widespread throughout Europe by the early Middle Ages and their prime object was the spiritual welfare of their members, in life and in death. They evolved into a fusion of trade association, friendly society, burial club, examining board, closed shop and job centre, and were as active in Zurich and Nuremburg as in Bristol, Edinburgh and London.

Every Company had its patron — St Thomas Becket for the Brewers, St Luke for the Butchers, the Blessed Mary for the Drapers, St Lawrence for the Girdlers, St Dunstan for the Goldsmiths and St Anthony for the Grocers. The Salters and the Skinners were the Fraternities of Corpus Christi, and the Parish Clerks, although not a Livery Company, are dedicated to St Nicholas. A unique Brotherhood are the pilots and seamen of the most Glorious and Undivided Trinity of Deptford Stronde, Trinity House.

All the Companies are linked to a particular City church, but the Solicitors are unique in holding their annual service in St Peter ad Vincula and their Election Court in the Queen's House, both within the Tower.

Many mottoes were in Latin, but some expressed practical English sentiments — 'True Hearts and warm Hands' for the Glovers, 'In the sweat of thy Brows shalt thow eate thy Bread' for the Gardeners, 'Within the Ark safe for ever' for the shipwrights, 'God can raise to Abraham children of Stones' for the Paviors, 'Weave Truth with Trust' for the Weavers and 'By Hammer and Hand all Arts do stand' for the Blacksmiths. The longbow was almost obsolete by 1488, but the Bowyers arms granted in that year carried the glorious battle honours — 'Crecy, Poitier and Agincourt'. Coats of arms were supported by a fantastic menagerie of lions, unicorns, panthers, elephants, camels, goats, rams, salamanders, seahorses, dolphins, swans, eagles and pelicans. The Needlemakers had a well stocked apple tree entwined with a serpent flanked by Adam and Eve in hand-stitched fig leaves, while on the Fruiterer's arms there was a tempting supply of apples but no figleaves.

The Skinners arms are of 'vair', meaning ermine, and Cinderella being a French lass had a cosy slipper of 'vair'. This was misheard by an English translator as 'verre', and thus was born the fairy story of the Glass Slipper!

There was no rhyme and little reason in the Court of Aldermen's 16th century division into Great Companies and Minor Companies. The Mercers' first charter is dated 1393, while that of the Weavers is 1155, and the Saddlers claim a lost one of 1272. But ever since 1515 the Lordly Mystery of the Mercers has ranked first of the Great Companies and the Clothworkers twelfth, with the Saddlers down at 25th, and the Weavers 42nd.

The Grocers rank second only the Mercers, and by the 13th century these Pepperers, who were wholesalers dealing 'in gross' had cornered the immensely profitable spice trade, and nine cloves and a camel feature on their coat of arms. Roman soldiers received part of their pay in salt, and the ninth place of the Salters among the Great Twelve testifies to its importance in the Middle Ages.

Elizabeth I granted the Feltmakers a charter which gave them the right to seize and burn impure imported hats, and they have always been known as 'Gentlemen Journeymen Hatters'

By 1709 some 76 Companies were recognized. There was a gap of exactly two centuries before the Solicitors were formed in 1909. The race is now on to become the 100th Company, and it will probably be won by the Information Technologists. Among recent foundations are the Marketors, Insurers, Engineers, Fuellers and Lightmongers. The 97th Company, is the Architects whose first Master, John Reid, has been Pageant Master of the Lord Mayor's Show for many years.

Many modern Companies are exclusive to their professions — the Guild of Air Pilots and Navigators, Accountants, Actuaries, Chartered Surveyors and Master Mariners. The Spectacle-makers are involved with opticians in the National Health Service, and the Apothecaries, who are a Society not a Company, have since 1617 issued diplomas to qualified medical practitioners and dispensers. The latest one is in sports medicine.

Some still have an important regulatory role — the Bakers, Brewers, Fishmongers, Goldsmiths, Gunmakers, Vintners.

Some have changed their role if not their name. The last of the 'old' Companies were the Fanmakers in 1709, when among those admitted was Sarah Ashton, fanmaker of Covent Garden. The modern Company now encourages Fan Engineering, and offers awards to students of heating, ventilating and air-conditioning.

Others are mainly concerned with administering their estates, schools and charities — the Clothworkers, Haberdashers, Mercers, Merchant Taylors, Skinners.

As late as the 1930s the Wheelwrights ruled their members with a rod of iron and a liveryman who insulted a government minister after a dinner at the Mansion House was asked to resign immediately. A float of 17th century wheelwrights plying their ancient craft with its spokes and felloes, hubs and axles, brought up the rear David Rowe-Ham's Show in 1986.

During the Industrial Revolution the Livery Companies developed an interest in further education and technical training, and this bore fruit in 1876.

Mayor Thomas Owden presided at the Mansion House when the City and Guilds of London Institute was formed to promote technical and scientific education. Whittington had been a Mercer with a keen interest in learning, and it was fitting that another Mercer, the Earl of Selborne, was elected first chairman of the new Institute. Since its foundation the Companies' support has run into millions of pounds, and the Lord Mayor and the Livery are still very much involved.†

Women have been members in their own 'wright' for centuries. Mention is made of three female Saddlers in 1537, around 1800 there was a free Sister of the Gunmakers and buxom tavern wenches have long been acceptable to the Innholders. Queen Bess was a free Sister of the Mercers, Edward VIII boasted "I am a Fishmonger". Princess Anne was the first lady Master of the Farriers.

Wives of Liverymen have always been welcome at the festive table, and the Grocers insisted that every member 'having a wife or companion should bring her to dinner, or une demoiselle in her place should she be ill or being great with child'. One gallant toast is to the 'Merry Maids, Good wives and Buxom Widows of the Bakers' Company'.

Only a Freeman could join a Company or hold any kind of civic office, vote in ward and Parliamentary elections and run a business. Added bonuses were exemption from market tolls and the grip of the Press Gang, the right of admittance to an almshouse in old age and, for the convicted Freeman, the choice of the rope or the axe for execution!

The three classes in a Company were Liverymen, Journeymen and Apprentices, the first two were Freemen, but only the Liverymen were of any consequence. 'Livery' in the Middle Ages meant an allowance of food and clothing to a retainer, a livery stable still provides that for horses, but in the City it now only gives the right to wear the Company's gown, badge, hood or hat. Only Liverymen can take part in Common Hall which meets in Guildhall to exercise their 'undoubted right' to elect the Lord Mayor and Sheriffs.

Then as now, there were four doors into the Freedom, and the Companies — Servitude, Patrimony, Honorary or Redemption. High sounding terms for apprenticeship, following in father's footsteps, becoming a conquering hero — or hard cash. The City Chamberlain, known as 'Mr Freedom' is in charge of all proceedings, and a hopeful applicant must be over 21, not an alien, bankrupt or convicted felon and good for £12. Two sponsors who are themselves Freemen must sign the nomination in the belief that the entrant will be a good citizen, and if all goes well the Freedom is granted in a colourful ceremony and an impressive certificate handed over.

One more name will be added to a Roll that goes back to 1275, and the first step has been taken on the road to become 'My Lord Mayor'.

†*The author's father and husband both graduated as engineers of City and Guilds.*

A thousand years of City Government

Guildhall

THE Saxon Court of Hustings was in the open air at Aldermanbury, and though Guildhall is first mentioned under Henry I it is probable that a stone building existed on the site before the Norman Conquest.

Alderman Fabyan wrote in his Chronicle in 1411 that 'ye Guyld Halle of London began to be new edyfied, and an olde and lytell cotage made into a fayre and goodly house'. Despite the passing of over five hundred years, the Great Fire and the Blitz, the alderman of Farringdon Without would have no difficulty in recognizing the Hall as 'it nowe apperyth'.

The work was finished under Henry VI and his arms are paired with Edward the Confessor's on the porch, a clue that the original Hall was indeed built before 1066.

By 1439 the roof was on, whether of timber or stone is still debated, and with the help of £35 from Whittington's executors the floor was paved with Purbeck marble. The total cost was enormous and the Companies were leaned on for benevolences, loans which they well knew were unlikely ever to be repaid. Henry V took an early interest in the work and gave 'free passage of lime, ragstone and freestone by land and water', and additional sums were raised by a certain amount of wrongful imprisonment and 'fines upon felons'.

Second only in size to Westminster Hall, it stood until consumed in the Great Fire 'in a bright shining coal as if it had been a pallace of gold or a great building of burnished brass'.

It was rebuilt on the existing crypts and walls, but with a temporary flat roof. Wren may have masterminded the restoration with the help of William Pope and Henry Hudson, carpenter and plasterer. Later a gothic facade was added by George Dance, architect of the Mansion House.

In the worst raid of the Blitz, 29th December 1940, gallant fire watchers dowsed any threatening incendiary bombs, but they were unable to stop flames spreading from adjacent buildings. Once again Guildhall was destroyed and the following morning the statue of Lord Mayor Beckford was seen undamaged amid the ruins, a light dusting of snow powdering his hair. Once more it was rebuilt on its sturdy foundations.

The Great Hall is entered from the west and measures 151ft.x49ft., and beneath the carpet are the standards of measurements, imperial and, since 1973, metric lengths. From the walls hang the banners of the Twelve Great Companies and the shields of over 80 others.

Gog and Magog

In the west gallery stand the Giants, successors to the bloodstained Gog and Magog who once dominated all City pageants. These 1953 replacements by David Evans stand 9ft. high in carved and gilded limewood and were the gift of Alderman John Wilkinson, Lord Mayor during the Blitz. Gog wields a morning star on a chain while Magog, dressed as a Roman centurion, carries a spear and shield decorated with a symbolic phoenix.

From the left of the door are statues of Winston Churchill by Oscar Nemon, unveiled in 1955. Nelson, who only appears on a medallion held aloft by mourning Britannia, Wellington, grasping a field-marshal's baton and attended by Peace and War and Pitt, Earl of Chatham. Opposite on the right side — William Pitt the Younger in his robes as Chancellor of the Exchequer, by E J C Bubb. Lord Mayor Sir William Beckford and the Royal Fusiliers, City of London Regiment and Boer War Memorial.

One 15th century window frame remains in the south-west corner, with the short standards of measurement on the adjacent sill. The names of all the Mayors of the past 800 years are inscribed on the windows above, and there is room for many more.

The Hall was much used by the Tudors and Stuarts for state trials, and a board lists many of those who went to their deaths after receiving doubtful justice in this court of law:

Anne Askew, age 25, 1546, burned at Smithfield protestant martyr: Henry Howard, age 29, 1547, son of Duke Norfolk, beheaded Tower Hill: Lady Jane Grey, age 16, 1554 beheaded Tower Green with her husband: Archbishop Cranmer 1556 burned at Oxford and Henry Garnett priest implicated in Gunpowder Plot, executed 1604

Guildhall hosted an infinite variety pre-1914 events all attended by the Lord Mayor of the day — in 1890 the Jubilee of the Penny Post; 1891 the Congress of Hygiene and Demography; 1900 the Institute of Journalists; 1901 a *Conversazione* for the Metropolitan Borough Councils; 1905 Freedom of the City bestowed on General William Booth of the Salvation Army; 1906 Iron & Steel Institute; 1907 the Dickens Fellowship; 1910 the Peace Society and in 1912 the Tonic Sol-Fa College.

The City's own 'democratic principles'

One Man, One Vote?

"The democratic principles which apply to the rest of the nation are not followed as closely in the City". The leader writer of the 'City Recorder' commenting on a ward election was putting it mildly, though his underlying point is cause for comment.

There are twenty five City Wards, and his attention had been alerted by the election of a new alderman for Candlewick, a contest won by a suburban solicitor who should have known a thing or two about the Representation of the People Act.

Not that there was any evidence of bribery of candidates, or intimidation or apathy among the electorate. On the contrary, there had been a 100% turnout at the poll with the winner scraping home by only one vote. He received seven votes, the runner-up six and the third, who may or may not have lost his deposit, polled five. Those eighteen votes represented the sum total of individuals entitled to vote for Candelwick's alderman.

This extraordinary state of affairs has come about due to demographic changes in the City, a place where half a million work and less than 10,000 live. None of the wards can honestly claim to provide a reasonable cross-section of Londoners. Walbrook, Lime Street and Dowgate can barely muster fifty voters, others are unbalanced by too many caretakers and police officers, Farringdon Without embraces all the lawyers in the Temple while the most populous wards of Cripplegate and Aldersgate include all the residents of the Barbican.

Minor tinkerings with the residential qualification have allowed some of those who rent garage space to vote, and also partners in professional firms, but not directors of limited companies. This has further unbalanced the electorate by including solicitors, accountants and surveyors but excluding bankers, property developers, shop assistants and company directors.

It is far easier to *stand* for election in the City than it is to *vote* in one, and if ever the old grievance of 'no taxation without representation' was justified it must apply to many large businesses in the Square Mile who pour millions of pounds into the Corporation's coffers every year.

The City used to have its own MP and in the past many a Mayor filled both offices, but in 1959 it was unwillingly united with Westminster to give a combined electorate of about 70,000.

The effect of the Community Charge on the City's franchise revenues has yet to be assessed, but the government must be uneasily aware that the Poll Tax of 1381 led to the Peasant's Revolt and the massacre of those responsible for its imposition!

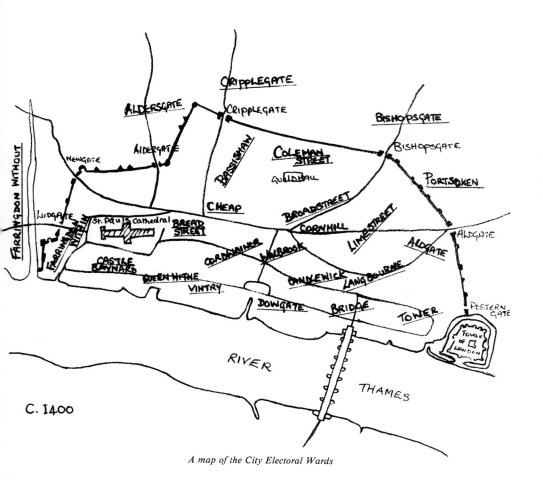

A map of the City Electoral Wards

London's Government

Common Council

THE full title of the Square Mile's governing body is the the 'Mayor, Aldermen and Commons of the City of London in Common Concil assembled'.

Members are not elected on a political ticket, so there is no party in power and no opposition. The Court consists of the Lord Mayor, 25 Aldermen and 130 Common Councilmen, each Ward having from four to six Councilmen, and one Alderman, and the former are elected annually at Ward Motes in December. The latter, formally elected for life, now have to retire at 70 like all other magistrates. The Lord Chancellor refused to exempt this last outpost of JP aldermen as a special case.

The Court of Aldermen meets once a month and among its powers is the appointment of the Town Clerk, the Recorder, and other officers. It deals with all matters concerning the Mayoralty, has a special relationship with the Commissioner of the City Police, maintains jurisdiction over the Livery Companies and has the right to veto the election of a new alderman. A veto that was exercised in 1973 against the first lady to be elected, and which provoked such outrage from all quarters that a few years later a different lady was quietly allowed to take her seat. *She* went on to become Lord Mayor in 1983, Lady Donaldson.

The Common Council is the local authority of the City and meets in Guildhall every third Thursday. It has full consultative and legislative powers, but meetings conducted by the Town Clerk are fairly brisk since the real work is done by committees, of which there are dozens.

The chairman of the City Lands Committee, known as the Chief Commoner, is Leader of the Council. Other important committees are the vital Coal, Corn and Finance Committee which manages the funds, the Policy and Resources Comitteeand the Irish Society, concerned with the City of Londonderry and the the estates in Ulster dating back to James I. Among others are the Gresham Committee, the Litter Act Committee, the Freedom Application Committee, the Traffic Management Committee, and the City of London (Arizona) Corporation.

More committees see to the spending of the rates on the City Police with its specialised Fraud Squad; public and environmental health including St Bartholomew's and St Mark's Hospitals; the City of London School, the City of London School for Girls, the Freemen's School in Surrey and the Guildhall School of Music and Drama; the Port of London and quarantine station at

Heathrow; the markets at Smithfield, Spitalfields and Billingsgate,(now on the Isle of Dogs); planning, engineering, architecture, communications and street cleansing; the Open Spaces that together with Epping Forest and Burnham Beeches cover 8000 acres; the Barbican Arts Centre, libraries and museums and the Golden Lane and Barbican Estates.

But where does the money come from?

The first source is the rates, and since these are levied on one of the most expensive acreages of real estate in the world, the income from the business rate is vast − £427m in 1987/1988.

Of this the City kept only £66m to finance its own services. £107m went into the national rate equalisation scheme; £212m to ILEA, the Inner London Education Authority; £21m to the LFCDA, London Fire and Civil Defence Authority and £20m to LRT, London Regional Transport.

Blackfriars, Southwark, London and Tower Bridge are maintained from the Bridge House Estates, originally money from the rents of houses on Old London Bridge. The Open Spaces, Markets and Schools are paid for from an ancient account called 'the City Cash', from which charitable donations in the City's name also come.

The Corporation is its own biggest landlord, and many of its holdings stem from medieval bequests of 'three tenements in the Shambles' or 'four dwellings in the parish of St Botolph'. These sites are now occupied by towering office blocks or the prestige head-quarters of international banks or oil companies, and the rents go to swell the City Cash.

Turtle soup may no longer feature at Mayoral banquets, but none of the lavish hospitality dispensed at Guildhall or the Mansion House or indeed the cost of the Mayoralty itself comes from the pockets of the ratepayers. That too is paid out of the coffers of the City Cash.

800 Years of 'My Lord Mayor'

Men of Mark

Eight hundred years of 'My Lord Mayor' and more than 600 First Citizens who have held that office have left an indelible mark on the City. A mark that covers a historic regiment, the famous schools founded by worthy Mayors, the Monument and London Bridge.

Coat of Arms

A Pikeman of the HAC

The Honourable Artillery Company

NO TROOPS may pass through the City without consent of the Lord Mayor, except for historical reasons the 3rd Battalion Grenadier Guards, 1st and 2nd Battalions East Kent Regiment The Buffs and the 6th Battalion Royal Fusiliers/City of London Regiment. Also the Royal Marines and the Honourable Artillery Company.

The Honourable Artillery Company, the oldest regiment of the Territorial Army, has provided a military escort for the Lord Mayor since the days of the Civil War. 'Pikeman' and 'Musketeer' are always among the traditional names of the Whitbread shires, and that pair are often among the six chosen to pull his coach in the Lord Mayor's show.

The HAC's charter of 1537 refers to the 'Fraternity or Guild of Artillery of Longbows, Crossbows and Handguns', firearms soon to be overtaken by the 'harquebus'. Milton, Wren and Pepys were all members, and today the Company has no difficulty drumming up volunteers from among the City's bankers and brokers, lawyers and liverymen, and the Queen is Captain-General of all these 'gentlemen of the Artillery Garden'.

The Train Bands were the forerunners of the HAC, and each Livery Company was obliged to furnish its quota of men to this citizen militia, some of the smaller companies being assessed at 'half a man'. In 1562 Mayor William Harper called a muster and ordered every man to repair to Leaden-hall in harness with pikes, guns, bows and bills, and wearing what passed for a uniform of a 'bluw clokes garded with red'. It was a purely routine occasion, and after marching to Moorfields for review by the Mayor the men dispersed to enjoy the rest of the day devoted to shooting contests, wrestling bouts and refreshment.

When John Norris, the finest soldier of his day, saw the motley throng of amateur soldiers at Tilbury boasting how they would repulse the veteran troops aboard the Spanish Armada he was appalled that 'no man England was afeared but himself'. The exact sentiments of the Duke of Wellington on the scum of the earth who made up his Infamous Army: 'I don't know about the enemy but, by God, they frighten me'.

In the Civil War another professional raged that the Dad's Army of a Militia was 'so transported by the jollity of the thing that no man was capable of the labour, care and discipline needed'.

Army rations were always one of the perks, and Mayor John Ireton's escort of the HAC in 1658 enjoyed the usual allowance of 'a pullet, a bottle of canary and a bottle of claret for each file of four men that marched'. Nor do the pikemen and musketeers of today go thirsty on returning to stack their arms at Whitbread's Brewery after the Show.

Schools and Colleges

LEARNING was the key that opened the door to advancement in the City, and many Mayors devoted their wealth to the foundation of new schools, colleges and libraries. Some, like Laxton, Judde and Sevenoke, remembered their country origins and founded schools at Oundle, Tonbridge and Seven-oaks, while others endowed schools in the City where they had made their fortunes.

St Anthony's where Thomas More was a pupil has vanished, but not the foundation of Whittington's friend the Common Clerk, who in 1442 left a bequest for the education of poor boys as choristers of Guildhall Chapel. Those 'Carpenter's children' have swelled to 800 at the City of London

Christ's Hospital

Christs Hospital Bandsman

School, which has recently moved into superb new premises south of St Paul's. Its old boys are Old Citizens and their association is the John Carpenter Club. The City of London School for Girls is in the Barbican.

Mercer Henry Colet served as Mayor from 1486 to 1495, a time when the Company was at its zenith, and his son put his inheritance into refounding St Paul's School in 1510.

At the time John Colet was Dean of St Paul's, and he revitalised the decayed cathedral school with three masters, a chaplain and 153 pupils, said to be the number of the miraculous draught of fishes. He left its management to the Mercer's Company with the backhanded compliment that 'though there was nothing certain in human affairs he yet found the least corruption in them'.

The Mercers as businessmen and the Dean as a scholar, were quick to appreciate the new printed books, and encouraged the first High Master of St Paul's to issue 'Lily's Latin Grammar'. This bane of schoolboys was not replaced at Eton until 1860, but at least by then all teaching was no longer in Latin or Greek.

Colet insisted that the children must pass an entrance examination, and forbade them to bring meat, drink or bottles into the school and waste no time breakfasting in the time of learning. 'Nor scorn what is done ignorantly nor any physical deformity'.

Colet's school eventually moved to Hammersmith and then over the river to Barnes close to its prep school, Colet Court. The new cathedral choir school was built in the Blitzed ruins of St Augustine with St Faith, its restored tower still acting as a slender counterpoint to the dome of St Paul's as Wren intended.

Another Mayor, Richard Dobbs, was praised by the Bishop of London because during Edward VI's short reign he 'didst win my heart for evermore, for that most blessed work of God, of the setting up of Christ's Holy Hospitals'

London's medieval hospitals being religious foundations had been in danger of extinction at the Dissolution of the Monasteries, but Henry VIII was persuaded to reinstate them and grant new charters. His frail son, for whom the doctors could do nothing, founded Christ's Hospital for the care and education of destitute children in the City.

Five years later Mary Tudor complained she did not "lyke the blewe boyes" who had usurped the place of the Franciscan monks, but a German visitor in 1599 was very impressed. "There were some 700 children kept there until fit for some craft or service ... fine children, taken from poor parents, and in one apartment 140 beds in a row either side where they sleep two and two together, and fewer girls in another room".

The school moved to Horsham in 1902, but the boys still by choice wear the Tudor blue cassock and bright yellow stockings, and the Blue Coat Girls have a harmonising uniform. The 100-strong Military Band has become traditional at the Lord Mayor's show.

Remembering 'the Great Fire'

THE Monument stands 202ft. tall, the distance from its base to the site of the shop owned by Thomas Farynor, baker to the King in Pudding Lane. The inscription commemorates the Great Fire which broke out 'in the dead of night, which, the wind blowing, devoured even distant buildings and rushed devastating through every quarter with astonishing swiftness and noise ... of the 26 wards, it utterly destroyed 15 and left 8 mutilated and half burnt. The ashes of the City covering as many as 436 acres'.

This slender candle of Portland stone credited to Wren, was actually designed by the City Surveyor, Robert Hooke. A plaque states it was begun with 'Sir Richard Ford being Lord Mayor of London in the year 1671; carried higher in the Mayoralties of Sir George Waterman, Sir Robert Hanson, Sir William Hooker, Sir Robert Viner and Sir Joseph Sheldon; and finished in the Mayoralty of Sir Thomas Davies in the year of the Lord 1677'.

In 1986, the quartercentenary of the Baker's Company, Lord Mayor Allan Davies and Master John Copeman unveiled a tablet on the wall of Lloyds Bank in Pudding Lane, the site of Farynor's shop. It replaced an earlier one of 1681 blaming the Papists for the outbreak and rejoicing that the arsonist had been hanged. This was later removed as being inaccurate, if not offensive, and can be seen in the Museum of London.

London Bridge

THE old nursery rhyme, and like many time-honoured children's verses is based on sound historic truth:

> *London Bridge is falling down, falling down, falling down,*
> *London Bridge is falling down, my fair lady*
> *Build it up with brick and stone, brick and stone, brick and stone,*
> *Build it up with brick and stone, my fair lady.*

Old London Bridge had spanned the Thames since Peter de Colechurch built it in 1176. The last dwellings and shops were removed in the 1760s, a parapet erected on both sides and the central arch widened. The opening of Westminster Bridge in 1749 had diverted much of the traffic away from the overcrowded old crossing, but the expanding City needed more than a single bridge and several prolonged winters further weakened the crumbling structure. By the beginning of the 19th century even the diehards had to admit it was unsuitable for horsedrawn vehicles and a hazard to shipping.

The Lord Mayor and Corporation were blamed for timidity and indecision over its fate, and an influential journal raged that the Bridge had cost the lives of perhaps a thousand people in its history and that 'this pernicious structure has wasted more money than would have sufficed to build a dozen safe and commodious Bridges'. Aldermen and turtles went together like steak and kidney, and another sneered that 'had a turtle or an alderman been lost' the old bridge would have been demolished years ago.

Eventually John Rennie's design was approved and on 18th June 1825, the 10th anniversary of Waterloo, the foundation stone was laid by Mayor Garrett wielding a silver trowel. The scaffolding was packed with the Nobility and Quality while over-loaded boats of spectators thronged the river and thousands more cheering people lined its banks. Flags flew from every rooftop, guns roared, several military bands competed against each other and the Monument was illuminated by gas flares. The spirit of the Thames was placated by crystal casket of gold coins and a copy of the 'Times' entombed beneath the foundation stone.

William IV and Queen Adelaide opened the new Bridge in August 1831, and under the Mayor John Key the City excelled itself with one of the last water pageants ever to grace the Thames. The royal party landed from their barge at Fishmongers Hall, crossed and re-crossed the bridge and then dined in state in a great tent erected along its length. Since the wide arches of the new bridge did not impede the river's flow there was never again a Frost Fair on the Thames.

Nelson's funeral barge had passed beneath Old London Bridge and, shortly before it was demolished and shipped to Arizona, Rennie's Bridge witnessed another funeral procession, Winston Churchill's. The Bridge saw the gaunt cranes along the Thames dip their jibs in silent homage to another national hero.

Lord Mayor Peter Studd opened the rebuilt bridge at Lake Havasu in 1971, and a pub called the 'City of London Arms', and in 1973 the Queen opened the third London Bridge accompanied by Lord Mayor, Lord Mais.

But Peter the Monk has not been forgotten, one of the new buildings on the Southwark approaches is called Colechurch House.

The Mark of Bridge House Estates

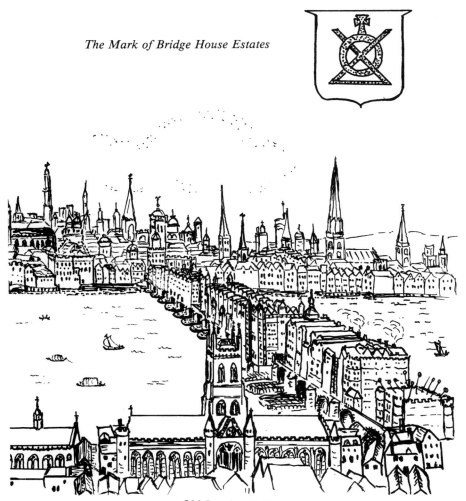

Old London Bridge

The early times – fixing the year

DATING THE MAYOR

IT is surprisingly difficult to give the exact dates for any early Lord Mayor, but remarkably easy to see why so many writers side stepped the problem by referring to him by his title, rather than his actual name.

Firstly, his mayoral year starts from the day he took office in late autumn, meaning that more than three quarters of it takes place the following year.

Secondly, the actual day of election varied over the centuries. In the very early days it was the day after the Feast of St Simon & St Jude, 28th October. Then in 1436 it changed to the saint's day of Edward the Confessor earlier in the month, before returning to 29th October.

Thirdly, although most of Europe followed the lead of Pope Gregory XIII and went over to the revised Gregorian calendar in 1582 by jumping from 4th to 15th October, England, ever out of step with its catholic neighbours across the Channel did not. Not until mid-18th century was the inaccurate Julian calendar abandoned, when it was felt that the change would no longer be seen as a devious popish plot.

By then the error stemming from the original calculations of Julius Caesar had grown into days, and Parliament decreed that New Year's Day should be set back from Lady Day, 25th March, to 1st January, and 3rd September 1752 should become 14th September. This finally put the calendar right with the seasons and Lord Mayor's Day moved from 29th October to 9th November, but it brought the mob out on the streets screaming 'give us back our eleven days'.

Pepys in the 1660s still celebrated the New Year on 25th March, but always spent a worrying day casting up his annual accounts on 31st December.

Here is just one example of the confusion inherited by future generations from the chaotic English calendar:

Charles I stepped out onto the scaffold in Whitehall on 30th January. Under the Old Style it was still 1648, but under the New Style that year had ended on 31st December, making the execution date in 1649. Even contemporary records found this confusing, and some records give it as 30th January 1648/1649.

It is therefore little help to dredge up the familiar dates of Bannockburn, Agincourt, Flodden and Waterloo as 1314, 1415, 1513 and 1815 without also knowing the month, even the day, in order to discover who was Lord Mayor of London during those stirring times.

So despite all attempts to *simplify* and unravel this tangled skein of dates, made worse by numerous Lord Mayors dying in office, errors will inevitably have crept into the text. The majority can be laid fairly and squarely at the doors of Julius Caesar and Pope Gregory!

Kings and Queens of England from 1066 and of
Wales from Edward I, Scotland from James I (James VI of Scotland)

(A spouse shown in parentheses was not the mother/father of the succeeding monarch)

NORMAN	1066	WILLIAM I	MATILDA
	1087	WILLIAM II	
	1100	HENRY I	(Adela of Lorraine)
	1135	STEPHEN	
PLANTAGENET	1154	HENRY II	ELEANOR of Aquitaine
	1189	RICHARD I	(Berengaria of Navarre)
	1199	JOHN	ISABELLA of Angoulême
	1216	HENRY III	ELEANOR of Provence
	1272	EDWARD I	ELEANOR of Castille
	1307	EDWARD II	ISABELLE of France
	1327	EDWARD III	(Philippa of Hainault)
	1377	RICHARD II	(Anne of Bohemia)
LANCASTER	1399	HENRY IV	MARY de Bohun
	1413	HENRY V	KATHARINE of Valois
	1422	HENRY VI	(Margaret of Anjou)
YORK	1471	EDWARD IV	ELIZABETH Woodville
	1483	EDWARD V	
	1483	RICHARD III	(Anne Nevill)
TUDOR	1485	HENRY VII	ELIZABETH of York
	1509	HENRY VIII	KATHARINE of Aragon, ANNE Boleyn, JANE Seymour, (Anne of Cleves, Katharine Howard, Katharine Parr
	1547	EDWARD VI	
	1553	MARY	(Philip of Spain)
	1558	ELIZABETH	
STUART	1603	JAMES I	ANNE of Denmark
	1625	CHARLES I	HENRIETTA MARIA of France
	1648	COMMONWEALTH	1659
	1660	CHARLES II	(Catharine of Braganza)
	1685	JAMES II	(Anne Hyde, Mary of Modena)
	1689	WILLIAM & MARY	
	1702	ANNE	(George of Denmark)
HANOVER	1714	GEORGE I	SOPHIA of Anhalt
	1727	GEORGE II	(Caroline of Anspach)
	1760	GEORGE III	CHARLOTTE of Mecklenburg
	1820	GEORGE IV	(Caroline of Brunswick)
	1830	WILLIAM IV	(Adelaide of Saxe-Meiningen)
WINDSOR	1837	VICTORIA	ALBERT of Saxe-Coburg
	1901	EDWARD VII	ALEXANDRA of Denmark
	1910	GEORGE V	MARY of Teck
	1936	EDWARD VIII	
	1936	GEORGE VI	ELIZABETH Bowes-Lyon
	1952	ELIZABETH II	PHILIP of Greece

Miscellany of Mayors

ASGILL – first to ride in the Lord Mayor's Coach
BARNE – switched from protestant Jane to catholic Mary
BECKFORD – backed the American rebels against George III
BILLESDON – was all at sixes and sevens
BLOODWORTH – was no match for a London in flames
BREMBRE – lynched by the mob for imposing the Poll Tax

Solicitors

ALLEN, JOHN 1525/1535 *Mercer* All Lord Mayors are weighed down by the memory of John Allen. After holding office twice, Allen died in 1545, and willed that 'the Lorde Mayre of London for the tyme being shall have my Collor of SS to use and occupie yearly ... and the same to remayne to hym and his successors mayres for the same effect'.

The chain of 26 gold links, interspersed with knots, roses and the Tudor portcullis was enlarged in 1567 for another Mercer, Roger Martyn, and has been worn by every mayor since.

ALLEYN, THOMAS 1659 *Grocer.* On 30 May 1660 the 'King came into his own again' and was welcomed back on his birthday by the deliriously cheering Londoners.

Not a Roundhead was to be seen, though many were still in power. But, so as 'never to go upon his travels again' Charles II would have supped with the devil himself. As the next best thing he dined with Mayor Alleyn, and then with the Liverymen at a series of Restoration Feasts. Many Companies had destroyed their decorations during the Commonwealth, and the Grocers had to borrow 'green men's shapes, periwigs and beards' from the Clothworkers to deck their own Hall for the King's visit.

Eager to show their loyalty the City Fathers gave him a valuable 'welcomm cuppe as is the custome'. They little dreamed that Charles would one day confiscate their precious charters and then force the hapless Companies to ransom them back.

ASGILL, CHARLES 1757 *Skinner.* For nearly fifty years after the unhorsing of Mayor Heathcote in 1710 his successors rode in a series of hired vehicles. Mayor Asgill was the first to use the new gilded coach, a wondrous conveyance sprung from a pumpkin in a fairytale which still rumbles through the City every Show Day.

It took until 1984 for Heathcote's humiliation to be forgotten, and then it was the Lady Mayoress, Sarah Traill, who made history riding side-saddle in the Lord Mayor's Show.

AUBREY, ANDREW 1339-40 *Pepperer* The brawling between the Guilds reached a climax when the Mayor and Sheriffs were set upon in Walbrook by the rival Skinners and Fishmongers. The outraged Aubrey had the ringleaders arrested, summarily tried in Guildhall and then beheaded in Cheapside.

He was commended by Edward 111, who had done much to encourage the religious Guilds and Fraternities to become more businesslike and less bellicose. Many Company charters date from his fifty year reign and a 1346 Act of Parliament ordered that all craftsmen should chose 'each his owne Mysterie', or mastery, and thereafter to acknowledge no other.

The King was admitted to the Linen Armourers, the tailors who made the padded garments knights wore beneath their chafing plate armour. Later known as Merchant Taylors they also produced military tents, and their arms show three 'imperial pavilions lined with ermine', replicas of those fanciful shelters that dotted the Field of the Cloth of Gold.

Sarah Traill - a break with convention

BARENTYN, DROGO 1398 *Goldsmith*
After profit the City preferred law and order above all else, and would back almost any strong man who kept the peace. Richard II's reign had dissolved into faction and tyranny, and under Barentyn the citizens transferred their allegiance and financial might to his cousin Bolingbroke.

As Henry IV he based his claim on descent from Edward III, what aspirant to the throne for the next century did not, and when faced with an uprising in favour of the deposed Richard the City stayed firmly behind the usurper, but not blindly.

"Sire,' the Mayor reminded him with a neat blend of self-interest, threat and flattery, "we have made you King, our King you shall be'.

BARNARD, JOHN 1737 *Glover − Grocer*
The Mayoralty has produced dolts and fools, knaves and rogues, but in a depraved age even the corrupt Prime Minister, Sir Robert Walpole, had to admit that this was a Mayor not to be bought. Possibly Barnard had no trouble resisting peculation or bribe taking, since he inherited and nurtured great wealth so he 'lived and died immensely rich'.

BARNE, GEORGE 1552 *Haberdasher*. Edward VI died at Greenwich in July 1553, a few days after the City Fathers had witnessed his secret will bequeathing the Crown to his protestant cousin, Lady Jane Grey. Five past, present or future Lord Mayors attested the document: John Gresham, Andrew Judde, Richard Dobbis, George Barne and Thomas Offley. It flouted the lawful succession but the Duke of Northumberland, Jane's father-in-law, held the whip hand and Barne shortly afterwards proclaimed her Queen.

The Londoners would have none of it. Much as they feared Mary, the Spanish "conduit by which the rats of Rome" would steal back into the kingdom, they believed in fair play and backed her against the usurper. Nine days later, Barne and his colleagues were again summoned, this time within the City. The nobility had already scuttled away from Jane's doomed cause, and the aldermen, seldom ones to rate valour higher than discretion, were quick discretion, were quick to follow them. Jane's own father proclaimed Queen Mary at Tower Hill, and Barne did the same at Paul's Cross.

With her half-sister Elizabeth riding at her side Mary paid a state visit to the City in August. Barne had prudently rounded up all anti-Spanish protesters, but still had to quell a riot around Pail's Cross when a catholic priest mounted the pulpit for the first time since the break with Rome. With dumb insolence the Londoners then took to staying away from the catholic services altogether until the exasperated Mayor was obliged to call on the 'ancients of the Companies to resort to the sermons lest the preachers be discouraged'.

Barne survived Mary's perilous reign, and saw his daughter married to Elizabeth's spymaster and unwavering Protestant champion, Sir Francis Walsingham.

BATEMAN, ANTHONY 1663 *Skinner* Bateman accepted a pension of 30 shillings a week from the Corporation after his business failed in 1665, although he eventually died in a debtor's prison. Perhaps the books were already in the red during his Mayoralty and he was trying to save on the catering, or else the silver had gone missing during the Commonwealth. Pepys had a good snoop round before the feast and noted a bill of fare under every salt cellar, but was peeved to see that only the Mayor's and the Lords' tables were set with napkins and knives. He sat at the Merchant Strangers' table where they had ten good dishes and plenty of wine, but found the occasion 'very unpleasing in that we had no napkins nor change of trencher, and drank out of earthen pitchers and ate off wooden dishes'.

He was lucky to have had a dinner at all for the next two feasts were cancelled due to the Plague. Even worse than Bateman's frugality was the squalor of another dinner which was the 'poorest, meanest, dirtiest table in a dirty house that ever I did see in any Sheriff of London, a plain, ordinary silly man, but rich'.

Benjamin Franklin

BECKFORD, WILLIAM 1762-1769 *Ironmonger*. Having been born and lived in Jamaica during his father's governorship Beckford probably had a better understanding of the New World than most of his fellow aldermen, or Parliament. An early supporter of the American Colonies, he backed Wilkes in his scurrilous press campaign against the government.

When a Common Council petition to George III was rudely ignored, Mayor Berkford retaliated. The King "stood speechless and there was trouble and agitation among his ministers and courtiers", but Pitt the Elder cried out that the "spirit of Old England spoke on that never to be forgotten day".

Beckford was a sick, old man, unwillingly serving a second term, and he died a month after that confrontation and before the Common Council voted funds for his statue in Guildhall.

Benjamin Franklin had lived and worked in the City, and when the War of Independence broke out he did not forget the friendship of Englishmen like Beckford and Wilkes. He sent an order to the Navy that should they meet the "great Discoverer Captain Cook, they were to offer him every aid and service, since it would ill become an American to lift their hands against one who had earned the reverence and gratitude of all mankind".

BILLESDON, ROBERT 1483 *Haberdasher.* The quarrels over precedence between the Skinners and the Merchant Tailors led to annual bloodshed in the Mayor's Pageante, and became positively lethal when the procession took to the Thames. The Company barges behaved like warships of opposing navies with the racing and ramming leading to 'many a drowning and sadde loss of lyfe'.

It took the Wisdom of a Solomon to put an end to these disputes, and Mayor Billesdon came up with a worthy judgement. He ordered that sixth and seventh places should alternate every year, with the Skinners giving a feast to their rivals on Corpus Christi Day and the Merchant Taylors welcoming them on St John the Baptist's Day. If either company should include the Mayor, then that year they should take precedence whether their turn or not. One account says that on the Thames they were ordered to row in the approved order, but be lashed together in amity as they approached Westminster.

'All at sixes and sevens' is said to stem from this event although Chaucer had used the phrase, but the Billesdon Award endures to this day. At their annual feasts the traditional toast is drunk 'Skinners and Merchant Taylors, Merchant Taylors and Skinners, Root and Branch may they flourish for ever'.

BIRCH, SAMUEL 1814, Cook. "Not tonight, Charles, I've got a headache". Tired of excuses from his mistress the King ordered up for her several 'hot invalide jellies'. Nell Gwynn was soon back to her seductive self, and the reputation of Mr Birch and Mr Horton of Cornhill was made.

By 1690 they were catering to the judges at

Old Bailey, and when Captain Cook entertained the Admiralty on board 'Endeavour' the dinner was ferried down the Thames from their kitchens.

A direct descendant, Samuel Birch, brought his nephew George Ring into the business, and during his Mayoralty the City was regaled with a stupendous Waterloo Feast. Colonel Birch was also commander of the Militia, but still managed to take time off from the kitchen and the parade ground to write poems and plays.

A clockmaker named Brymer joined the partnership in the 1830s and Queen Victoria's Coronation Banquet, punctual to the minute, ran to sixty courses. Ring & Brymer are now specialist caterers within Trusthouse Forte, and nearly three centuries after Nell Gwynn's sampling of Mr Birch's restorative jelly another member of his company hosted the Lord Mayor's Banquet, Lindsay Ring in 1975.

BLOODWORTH, THOMAS 1665 *Vintner.* Pepys kept a diary, Bloodworth did not, and he is damned forever in Sam's pages as 'a silly man', and one who after noting the early flames in Pudding Lane on 3rd September 1666 had climbed back into bed scoffing that 'a woman could piss it out'. Later that morning Pepys met the Mayor with a handkerchief around his neck crying like a fainting woman " what can I do? I am spent, people will not obey me, I have been pulling down houses but the fire overtakes us faster than we can do it".

Charles II viewed the blaze from the Mayor's Livery Hall, but within hours Vintners Hall had gone too. By next day Bloodworth had been relieved of his duties and overall command given to the Duke of York, the Lord High Admiral. At Pepys' suggestion seamen from Deptford and Woolwich were brought in to create firebreaks by blowing up houses, but it was the dropping of the galeforce east wind that saved what was left of the City.

It was not much. Within the old walls the devastation stretched from the Tower to the Temple, and from the Thames to Smithfield — 13,000 houses, 87 churches, 44 Livery halls, St Paul's, Guildhall and the Royal Exchange were all gone.

Bloodworth's own house was destroyed, but in November he handed over the government of the ruined City to Mayor William Bolton and retired into obscurity, but not out of reach of the merciless Pepys. In December he met 'my late Lord Bloodworth, under whom the City was burned. But, Lord, the silly talk that this silly fellow had. A very weak man he seems to be.'

Bloodworth's efforts to justify his actions in print found few sympathisers, but he does seem to have found comfort in his Company and many fellow Vintners ready to agree that in 'the severest year that ever man did' endure, that he had done his best, ineffectual though it had been. Others damned him with even fainter praise for being 'willing though it may be not very able to do great things'. He even failed his daughter by marrying her to Judge Jeffries, soon to be vilified as the Hanging Judge of the Monmouth Rebellion.

BOLEYN, Geoffrey (Bullen) 1457 *Mercer.* A hatter and then a mercer, he was the great-grandfather of Anne Boleyn, second wife of Henry VIII. Nelson was proud to claim decent from this Lord Mayor, through Anne's sister, Mary Boleyn.

BOLLES, GEORGE 1617 *Grocer* Even the first of the Stuarts rubbed the City up the wrong way, and James I, who could not have been ignorant of custom, was affronted to be stopped by the Lord Mayor at Temple Bar. Bolles, ceremonial sword in hand, stood barring his into the City until the traditional courtesies had been exchanged. "Whisht," James muttered, "I had thought there was no king in England save myself".

He might have been James VI in Scotland, but to the English he was merely James I and a poor successor to Great Harry's daughter, Elizabeth. The City's independence riled him on another occasion when he demanded a loan of £20,000 and the aldermen retorted that they could not lend what they had not got. Tempers rose on both sides, with the King finally threatening to ruin the City by removing the Court, the law courts and the Parliament to Oxford. "You are at liberty to remove yourself and your courts wheresoever you please," came the Mayor's suave reply, "only we pray you to leave to us the Thames".

Ludgate in the Great Fire

BOLTON, WILLIAM 1666 *Merchant Taylor* The ashes of the Great Fire were barely cold before plans for a new City were laid before the King. A multitude of cranks rushed in with preposterous schemes, but Christopher Wren and John Evelyn produced designs which would have resulted in one of the most elegant townscapes in Europe. Sadly they had reckoned without the vested interest of all those who had lost their homes and businesses, and were not prepared to see the sites disappear beneath Italianate piazzas and colonnaded terraces.

The team of Fire Court judges sitting in Cliffords Inn had the monumental task of assessing claims and settling disputes, and of Wren's grand design only St Paul's and his incomparable churches were ever completed. New building regulations specified stone, brick and tile in place of inflammable timber and thatch, but the powerful landlords won the right to rebuild on the old medieval pattern of narrow streets. Lovat Lane off Eastcheap still has its central runnel, the primitive drainage system that ran down into the Thames. Unlike many recent Mayors Bolton was no chartered accountant, and was ousted from the chair for failing to account for £1800 of the funds collected for victims of the Fire. Possibly it was muddle rather than fraud, for when he fell on hard times he was paid a pension of £3 a week, three times more than paid out to Bateman.

BOWATER, THOMAS VANSITTART 1913 *Girdler* On 23rd August 1914 the Royal Fusiliers, City of London Regiment, mustered in the Temple Gardens before marching to the Tower where the Mayor administered the Oath of Allegiance.

Later, with the army in retreat from Mons, Bowater welcomed Prime Minister Asquith and Winston Churchill to Guildhall to launch Kitchener's Recruiting Scheme – 'Your Country Needs YOU'.

A record number of four Bowaters have served as Lord Mayors of London – Thomas in 1913, Frank in 1938, Ian in 1969 and Noel in 1953. In 1913 Ian Bowater had been a pageboy to his uncle, and when he became Lord Mayor in 1969 his page was his grandson, John Doughty, taking his first steps along the family's traditional path.

BOWES, MARTIN 1545 *Goldsmith.* He added a jewelled pendant to the Mayor's gold chain of double 'SS, but this cross of pearls and precious stones has disappeared without trace.

The Reformation had not changed things overnight, and the Friday fast day was still widely observed. To protect the fishing and shipbuilding trades as much as to follow the rules of the Church, there had once been 150 fish days to 215 flesh days.

Bowes was empowered to enforce the Lenten rules, and a Hammersmith housewife and a Smithfield man were punished 'by judgment of my Lord Mayor' for eating forbidden meat. They had to ride through the 'markettes of the Citie, having a garland on theyr heades of the pyges pettie toes and a pygge hanginge on each of theyre brestes'. Sellers of rotten fish suffered the same punishment with 'stinkynge fysshe and oisters' hung round their necks while they were paraded through Billingsgate.

Bowes was proud of his name and every year presented to the prize scholars of St Anthony's School, the Tantony Pigs, silver bows and arrows. His punning coat of arms, a *rebus*, of three red bows on a field of ermine appears in the arms of the Queen Mother, born Lady Elizabeth Bowes-Lyon.

Clothworkers

The English have a taste for verbal gymnastics, and other Mayors providing scope for play on their names have been Welles, Key, Bridge, Fox, Ring and Cork.

Bowes left a bequest to the Goldsmiths for a sermon on St Martin's day, and for the upkeep of the banners and fabric of his tomb in St Mary Woolnoth where he lies beside his three wives, Cecily, Anne and Elizabeth.

John Boydell

BOYDELL, JOHN 1790 *Stationer*. Engraved and printed collections of popular paintings in competition with the traditional imported French prints. His illustrated Shakespeare was an instant best-seller, and the total English exports of fine engravings to the continent soon reached £100,000 annually.

Boydell's trade was ruined by the Napoleonic Wars. 'Anxious to discharge my debts at the advanced age of eighty-five' he appealed to Parliament to be allowed to dispose of his prints and paintings by lottery, and all the tickets had been sold and his estate saved from bankruptcy by the day he died.

BRANCHE, JOHN 1580 *Draper* Branche may have been 'feeble in health', but he gave a dusty answer to the Privy Council when it complained that the 'ancient and honourable Feast' had been discontinued without consulting them.

That year the "Lord Mayor's Day was a Fast Day, a Fish Day, so the Feast could not be a seemly one" Branche pointed out haughtily, "nor was it usual to obtain permission of Her Majesty or the Privy Council to omit any function from the City's calendar".

BREMBRE, NICHOLAS 1383-85 *Grocer.* The aggressive Grocer had been a King's man during the Peasant's Revolt, and was knighted by Richard II for curbing the ambitions of his uncle, John of Gaunt.

But Brembre had few friends among the people having deposed the popular Mayor Adam Stable, and when he re-imposed the hated Poll Tax which had caused the revolt, the mob turned on him. He was given a mockery of a trial and then hanged, drawn and quartered.

New taxes have always fuelled revolt in England, and two other victims by the anti-Poll Tax protesters were the Archbishop of Canterbury and the Lord Treasurer, forerunner of the Chancellor of the Exchequer!

BROWN, STEPHEN 1438/1448 *Grocer* Several bad harvests, a severe drought and the continual drain of the French Wars led to a famine in Brown's first Mayoral year. Caxton recorded that 'Steven Brown, at that time mayer of London, sent into Prussia and brought to London shippes laden with rye, which eased and did much good to the people, for corne was so skarce that in some places poor people made them brede of fern rootes.'

BROWNE, RICHARD 1660 *Woodmonger – Merchant Taylor*. The Restoration was only five months old, and the oak tree at Boscobel in which Charles had hidden after the disastrous Battle of Worcester was the centrepiece of Browne's Show.

On St George's Day, 23rd April, the following year Charles II was crowned in the Abbey with all the old ritual and magnificence. True to tradition the monarch had set out to his coronation from the Tower and in the procession was Mayor Browne carrying the Crystal Sceptre. Two knights in the ancient splendour of the Dukes of Normandy and Aquitaine and Garter King of Arms went ahead of him, and he was followed by the Duke of York and the Lord High Constable of England. The Mayor's importance is shown by his closeness to four great nobles and the King.

Despite the welcome pageantry, discontent and danger simmered beneath the surface calm, and Browne had great difficulty in keeping the peace in the City. Disbanded soldiers rioted for their arrears of pay, while the worst threat came from the extreme Puritan Fifth Monarchists calling on their supporters to rid the nation of the Stuart Anti-Christ and prepare the way for the Second Coming.

Pepys was dismayed at having no powder for his pistol, but apprehensively donning his sword went forth with Alderman Ford, Mayor in 1670, and saw the 'streets full of train-bands and a great stir. What mischief these rogues have done, I think near a dozen killed this morning on both sides. The shops shut up and all things in trouble'. The revolt was suppressed after a few days and the Fifth Monarchy leaders executed as traitors.

Samuel Pepys

Charles II

Miscellany of Mayors

Gardners

CHIGWELL – 'the vilest worm'
CLOPTON – the family that featured in Shakespeare
DAKIN – taken for a ride by an aristocratic 'con' man
DUCKETT – the unacceptable face of Tudor capitalism
DONALDSON – the unique 656th Lord Mayor

CAMBELL, JAMES 1629 *Ironmonger.* Several harvests failed in the 1620s, France and Spain were at daggers drawn, the Thirty Years war was ravaging northern Europe and Plague was stalking the land.

The Companies were asked to cut back on feasting and donate the savings into a fund for Plague victims. Cambell set a good example at Guildhall, and even the convivial Vintners invited no guests to their election dinner. Nobody may have benefited from this austerity since it was paid for by the Renter Wardens, but next year when the Vintners rationed themselves to only wine and cakes the Sick did receive £10.

CHICHELE, ROBERT 1411-1421 *Grocer.* The Chicheles were originally North-amptonshire farmers and generations of them served the City and the nation. Robert's brother Henry was Archbishop of Canterbury, another brother William was Sheriff. His nephew John was Chamberlain and a Sheriff, but still found time to father twenty four children.

The monarchs frequently turned to the City for loans, and if these were not always repaid in cash at least some favours were done in return. Henry V1 put in a good word for one of John's ten sons with the ruler of Ferrara, the Marquis d'Este, and so glowing

was the recommendation that the Mayor's unknown nephew was appointed Rector of the University.

Robert left an endowment for a banquet on the anniversary of his death for 2400 poor householders of the City, with twopence each in addition. His house in Harp Lane was on the site of the present Baker's Hall, and St Stephen Walbrook, parish church of the Mansion House, was built on land bequeathed by Chichele.

CHIGWELL, HAMO de 1319 *Pepperer.* Hard words were as common as blows in Plantagenet London, and a defeated mayoral rival cursed Chigwell as 'the vilest worm that had been in the City for more than 20 years, a blessing if his head were severed from his body'.

CHIVERTON, RICHARD 1657 *Skinner.* The right royal cortege of the Lord Protector Cromwell wound its ceremonial way to Westminster Abbey in October 1658. The crown, orb and sceptre lay on a bed of velvet, and the Clothworkers had supplied the banners, standards and 'all the taffeta and fringe that was used' to the tune of £164. An armoured knight headed the long line of soldiers and citizens who included Chiverton and the aldermen, a number of whom were Councillors of State.

CLAYTON, ROBERT 1679 *Scrivener – Draper.* John Evelyn took the Countess of Sutherland to dine with the Mayor so she could see that none of his predecessors had exceeded this 'Prince of Citizens for the stateliness of his palace, prodigious feasting and magnificence.'

The diarist mixed easily with the highest in the land, but that night he enthused that the 'feast and entertainment might have become a King. The pomp and ceremony of such an hospitable custom and splendid magistrature does no city in the world shew'.

CLOPTON, HUGH 1491 *Mercer.* Hugh left home for London to become a Mercer, the City MP and then Mayor, but he never forgot Stratford-on-Avon. He died a bachelor and is buried in London, not as he wished in the Clopton Chapel in Stratford, but the 14-arched stone Clopton Bridge he built in his birthplace still spans the Avon.

Shakespeare's father was a tradesmen and the Cloptons were gentry, but Will would have known them and may have used Clopton House as the setting for the 'Taming of the Shrew'. There are several other clues linking the family to his plays. A lovesick girl who drowned herself in the Avon was actually Margaret Clopton, but surely in 'Hamlet' she is immortalised as Ophelia?

CROSBY, BRASS 1770 *Goldsmith.* A champion of freedom of speech along with Wilkes and Beckford. Parliamentary debates were never published, and when reports of speeches in the House of Commons, of which Crosby was a member, went on sale the government ordered the arrest of the printers. Crosby refused, and when a Commons servant of the Speaker came in person to arrest them the Mayor had the man taken into custody and charged with assault.

For defying the privilege of Parliament, Crosby and Alderman Oliver MP, were sent to the Tower. A mob of 50,000 turned out in the streets, broke the Prime Minister's windows and catching sight of him grabbed his hat and tore it to shreds. The government backed down and released the aldermen who were hailed with 'loud and universal huzzas

as the guardians of the City's rights and of the nations's liberties'.

Crosby had come to London in 1725 from Staffordshire as an ambitious attorney, and married three wealthy widows in succession. He purchased the office of City Remembrancer for £3,600, was elected alderman and Sheriff, and followed the Anglo-American Barlow Trecothick as Lord Mayor.

In January 1772 the Corporation and City voted a 'Silver Cup of the value of 200 Pounds to Brass Crosby Esq. our late Worthy Lord Mayor for the noble stand he made in the business of the Printers'. The other two champions were given silver cups at half the price, and though Wilkes' has vanished, Crosby's was presented to the City in 1935 by Lord Wakefield, *(Lord Mayor 1915).*

CUBITT, WILLIAM 1860-61, *Fishmonger.* Lord John Russell had finally retired as City MP but Cubitt's hopes of replacing him at Westminster came to nothing, and as a consolation prize he was re-elected for a second term, a unique event in modern times. As Lord Mayor he opened the Mansion House Lancashire Relief Fund to help the destitute cotton spinners thrown out of work by the American Civil War.

He was a founder of the firm of building contractors who changed the face of Victorian London and sprawled it out into the suburbs. Joseph Cubitt, of London, Chatham and Dover Railway fame, designed the second Blackfriars Bridge and Queen Victoria had a busy day opening it, and Holborn Viaduct, on the same day in 1869.

William Curtis

CURTIS, WILLIAM 1795 *Draper* An eccentric who may have got on well with the increasingly mad George III. In honour of the King's visit to Scotland Curtis had his own portrait painted in Highland costume, attired in the full glory of eagle feathers, sporran and tartan socks, and brandishing a petition from the burgesses of Inverness.

He was a sugar baker by trade, a High Tory by conviction and out of step with most of the radical aldermen. In the public interest he once fined himself for a dirty pavement outside the Mansion House.

DAKIN, THOMAS 1870 *Spectaclemaker.* The sufferings of the Parisians during the Franco-Prussian War were heartrending, and when the Marquis de Morancy approached Mayor Dakin on behalf of his starving countrymen £500 was pressed into his grateful hands. He was also invited to address a public meeting.

The donation and the Marquis' speech were reported in the 'Times' and alerted the French embassy to this hitherto unknown nobleman claiming to be the Mayor of Chateaudun. He proved as elusive to track down as his title, and was only unmasked many years later when arrested elsewhere for a less successful confidence trick.

The generosity of Londoners to the victims of natural catastrophes and human tragedies was proverbial, and as Chief Almoner the Lord Mayor headed all fund raising efforts. There was no social security and very few insurance schemes at the time, and millions of pounds were raised over the years for mining disasters, floods, hurricanes and shipwrecks. Much of it came in sixpences and shillings dropped into collecting boxes outside the Mansion House, and these had to be emptied hourly for the 'Titanic' appeal.

DASHWOOD, FRANCIS 1702 *Vintner.* 'Sir Samuel Dashwood's Triumph' was a notable event, and he was the first of six Vintner Lord Mayors in the 18th century. St Martin is the Company's patron saint, and scarlet-cloaked on a white horse he lead the pageant of satyrs, halberdiers, Roman lictors and assorted cripples and beggars. The cha-

riot of Ariadne drawn by two live panthers and the galleon of Bacchus aroused deafening cheers, much encouraged by the lavish distribution of wine along the way.

Queen Anne and her stolid husband, George of Denmark, watched the Show in Cheapside and then attended the Guildhall banquet under a lofty Imperial canopy. She knighted the Mayor and several other gentlemen as well as a linen-draper, plain Mr Eaton, from whose shop she had watched the procession pass. The assembled Vintners sang an ode composed by the City's poet.

DODMER, RALPH 1529 *Brewer — Mercer* An early rebel against the dominance of the Great Twelve, and one who refused to translate to one of them on election. A spell of imprisonment and a heavy fine made him change his mind, and his affiliation from Brewer to Mercer.

At his banquet the peers sat at a separate table headed by Henry VIII's new Lord Chancellor, Thomas More. As a boy Henry had been presented with a pair of gilt goblets, for which he had thanked the 'Fader Maire and Brethren' and hoped that in time to come he would not forget 'this greate and kynd remembraunce'. The City in its turn was always quick to incline to the Royal Will, and though nobles, bishops, heretics, wives and Lord Chancellors paid with their lives for falling foul of Henry's temper, no mayoral career was abbreviated on a Tudor scaffold.

Quality control is nothing new, and as a Brewer Dodmer would have seen to it that the aleconners were up to the job. Tavern keepers caught watering the beer or serving short measure were fined and jailed, and had their fraudulent measures publicly burned. An alewife found using pitchers with 'naughtie bottommes' was sent to 'to play bo pepe thorawe a pillory'

A wine merchant who sold 'red wine which was unsound and unwholesome for man, in deceit of the common people in contempt of our Lord the King, and to the shameful disgrace of the officers of the City' was put out of business. He was compelled to drink a draught of it, had the rest poured over his head and was forced to forswear the calling of a Vintner in the City of London for ever.

Lady Donaldson

DONALDSON, MARY 1983 *Gardener.* The 656th Mayor, but the first lady to hold the office. A true high-flyer of a Lord Mayor she took to the skies on Ascension Day in a hot air balloon to raise funds for the NSPCC.

The Post Office produced a first day cover for her Show and Cant's of Colchester named a pink rose after her. She planted the first bushes of 'Mary Donaldson' in the gardens around St Paul's.

"I was taught that everything had to be earned," she once said in an interview, "a lesson that has stood me in good stead". During the War she married a soldier, exchanging her nurse's uniform for a borrowed wedding dress, and nearly forty years later they achieved the unique partnership of Master of the Rolls and Lord Mayor of London.

Keen sailors, the Donaldsons were once shipwrecked in the Bay of Biscay but were plucked from the sea by some French fishermen and taken ashore. The local mayor noted down the incident as the rescue of two 'distressed British seamen'.

DUCKETT, LIONEL 1572 *Mercer.* In his portrait Duckett looks out on the world as the Tudor version of the 'unacceptable face of capitalism'. Hard-eyed, and tight-lipped beneath the pointed beard, his 'fat cat' image is enhanced by the sleek luxury of a furred gown and gold collar.

He was Thomas Gresham's partner in the Royal Exchange, and a mine owner in Cumberland and Germany. He had plump fingers in many other commercial ventures, two of the most profitable being slave trading and piracy, both highly respectable professions for venture capitalists in Elizabethan England. Rich and miserly, Duckett added to his money bags by marrying the widow of another wealthy alderman.

Sir Lionel Duckett, financed the slave trade

DUNCOMBE, CHARLES 1708 *Goldsmith.* Charlie, a young apprentice, fought his way through the rush hour crowds on London Bridge every morning, never knowing as he ran past St Magnus the Martyr whether he was already late for work. After yet another thrashing he vowed that if ever he became Lord Mayor he would present the church with a clock to save other boys from a hiding.

He kept his word, and the clock projecting over Lower Thames Street is dated 1709 and was the gift of Lord Mayor Duncombe. In the 1930s the bulk of Adelaide House was allowed to hide Wren's beautiful steeple, so once more workers hurrying over the bridge are at a loss to know the time.

Miscellany of Mayors

E-H

FITZAILWYN – the first 'Mair' of London
FITZTHOMAS – died in the Tower for the City's rights
HARDEL – built a cage for the king's elephant
HEATHCOTE – fell off his horse in his own Show
HOUBLON – first governor of the Bank of England

Haberdashers

EDWIN, HUMPHREY 1697 *Barber – Surgeon – Skinner* The Mayor would have wielded a scalpel as readily as a razor, and his Company spent much time pursuing quacks who set up as rivals to their own brutal surgery. It finally took an Act of Parliament to ensure that 'no butcher, tailor, waxchandler or other person is to cut, dissect or embalm any dead body'!

Despite the Muscovy Company, any Russian was still a novelty and Peter the Great created a sensation at Mayor Edwin's feast. He also created havoc in John Evelyn's garden in Deptford by pushing his drunken mates through the magnificent holly hedge in a wheelbarrow, and by his personal habits in the house which were 'right nasty'. Evelyn called in his friend Christopher Wren to help his gardener assess the damage, and then submitted a bill for £150 to the Treasury.

EYRE, SYMON 1445 *Draper* After serving seven years as an apprentice Eyre discovered his master was an upholsterer, not a draper. With great difficulty and expense he found a new master, and then had to serve another seven years before becoming a journeyman Draper.

The long training must have paid off for he became a wealthy merchant with a mansion alongside the foreign bankers in Lombard

Symon Eyre

Street, and his son married the daughter of Robert Large, Mayor 1439. Eyre was famed for his charity, and he built and stocked a granary in Leadenhall to sell corn cheaply when poor harvests threatened famine. The retail market at Leadenhall is built on the site of Eyre's granary which itself stood, unknown to him, on the ruins of the Roman forum.

FITZAILWYN, HENRY 1189-1211 *Mercer* The first 'Mair', appointed by Richard I. When the Lionheart was imprisoned it was Fitzailwyn who imposed a tax on the Londoners to raise the ransom. William FitzOsbert, a popular figure known as Longbeard, refused to pay up, incited others to resist and when threatened with arrest fled with his followers to the sanctuary in St Mary le Bow. They were smoked out, and when they emerged scorched and choking they were seized and dragged to Tyburn.

This impious breach of sanctuary by the Mayor's men shocked the Londoners, and for a while Longbeard was hailed as a saint. Splinters from the scaffold were treasured as holy charms to cure the sick but his cult soon faded, unlike that of his contemporary Thomas Becket who was born within sight of St Mary le Bow.

Fitzailwyn died in office after nearly twenty years and was succeeded by another Mercer, Roger Fitzalan from 1212-1214.

FITZTHOMAS, THOMAS 1261-64 *Guild unkown* A Queen with hordes of grasping relatives always meant trouble and Henry III, coming to the throne aged nine, was first dominated by his advisers, and then by his wife, Eleanor of Provence. She was so hated that once her barge had to turn back to the safety of the Tower when the Londoners pelted it with offal and stones from London Bridge. After forty years of misrule the citizens of Southwark opened the drawbridge to allow Simon de Montfort and his army to enter London. Backed by Mayor FitzThomas and the aldermen de Montfort then called the first truly representative Parliament in 1265.

Fitzailwyne

It was short-lived, and when de Montfort was killed at Evesham the King turned his vengeance on those who had defied him. FitzThomas tried to negotiate, but with the brave challenge that only so long 'as unto us you will be a good lord and King, will we be faithful and duteous unto you'. He swiftly became the first, but not the last, Mayor to be thrown into the Tower, where he died.

FLUDYER, SAMUEL 1761 *Tyler – Clothworker* A fervent King's man in a City growing increasingly pro-American, Fludyer made a great show of presenting George III with a Loyal Address on the birth of George, Prince of Wales, in August 1762. Wilkes and his faction were not impressed by the Mayor's enthusiasm, and blamed it on stupidity rather than conviction since:

His eye, in a fine stupour caught Implied a plenteous lack of thought'.

FOWLER, ROBERT 1883 *Spectaclemaker.* The first Quaker to benefit from the lifting of the ban on religious dissenters. A classical scholar he quoted passages from the 'Illiad' at his Mayoral Banquet, in the original Greek.

GAYER JOHN 1646 *Fishmonger.* The 'Lion Sermon' is heard every October in St Katharine Cree, Leadenhall Street in fulfillment of a Lord Mayor's vow.

Traveling in Turkey for the Levant Company Gayer once came face to face with a lion, and falling to his knees he begged the Lord to spare him. Miraculously the lion lost its appetite and failed to eat him, and on his return home Gayer endowed an annual lecture to be given forever in gratitude for his escape. A recent preacher was Terry Waite, soon to be held hostage himself in the Middle East.

Gayer was no coward, having seen service as a Colonel of the Train Bands from 1639-1642, a sure sign of martial spirit and good fellowship in the City. In Cowper's rollicking poem a century later:

> John Gilpin was a citizen, of credit and renown A train-band captain eke was he, of famous London Town'.

GISORS, JOHN de 1311-1312 *Pepperer.* Queen Isabella wrote from Windsor in November 1312 announcing the birth of a son, who would grow into the mighty Edward III. The arrival of an heir to the throne was cause for rejoicing in troubled times, and 'the Mayor, richly costumed, and the Aldermen arrayed in like suits of robes with the Drapers, Mercers and Vintners in costumes, rode on horseback to Westminster and there made offering, and then went in carols throughout the City, all the rest of the day and great part of the night'.

The rejoicings lasted for a week with a solemn service in St Paul's and a sumptuous feast in Guildhall, 'excellently well tapestried and dressed out' for the occasion.

Unfortunately the City was still dealing with Edward II, and when he sent a curt demand for troops and money it was equally curtly refused. The Mayor was deposed but before his arrest he was able to hand over the keys to the aldermen, so when a Bishop was set up in his place he was unable to take control. The mob attacked the Bishop and his brother in St Paul's, dragged them to the Standard in Cheape and after hacking off their heads threw the bodies into the town ditch.

No tears were shed by the aldermen when Edward II was 'most foully done to death' in a dungeon of Berkeley Castle in 1327.

GLYN, RICHARD 1758 *Salter.* Fortified by pints of Whitbread export beer the British troops stormed the Heights of Abraham at Quebec in 1759, a triumph muted by the death of General James Wolfe in the moment of victory.

The whole of Canada would soon be theirs, and only New Orleans and the swamps of Louisiana would be left of France's Empire in North America.

Glyn led the sombre rejoicings in the City, and it was his successor, Mayor Thomas Chitty, who offered a Loyal Address to George II on the fall of Montreal the following year. A few days later the King was dead and Chitty proclaimed his grandson from the Royal Exchange, 'God save King George III'

Financiers were a more cautious breed after the scandal of the South Sea Bubble in the 1720s, and private joint stock banks mushroomed. Richard Glyn was a dyestuffs merchant before becoming a partner in the Vere, Glyn and Halifax Bank in 1753. His son, also Richard Glyn and Lord Mayor in 1798, saw the bank prosper, and after various mergers it turned into Glyn, Mills, then Williams & Glyns and finally in 1985 amalgamated with the Royal Bank of Scotland.

GURNEY, RICHARD 1641 *Clothworker.* It had not yet come to Civil War when Gurney took office, but several aldermen had seen the inside of the Tower on the King's writ and the City was strongly for the Parliament.

On his return from a disastrous visit to Scotland, Charles I called at Guildhall. After promising to govern within the law and to uphold the Protestant faith 'if need be to the hazard of my life', he invited the Mayor and the Corporation to Whitehall Palace next day. There he knighted Gurney and those of the aldermen who had attended him.

But in January he stormed back to Guildhall demanding the surrender of five MPs who had defied him. Gurney, Alderman Pennington and others refused in the name of the privilege of Parliament and the rights of the City. Then, to rub in their independence they had the MPs escorted back to Westminster by the Train Bands. At the request of the Commons the soldiers thereafter mounted a daily guard on the House.

By August civil war was inevitable, and Gurney knew where his ultimate loyalty lay. Control of the Train Bands was vital, but when he read out the Commission of Array calling the City to arms in the King's name he was deprived of his office. Isaac Pennington was appointed in his place, and proclaimed the Militia Ordinance in the name of the Parliament. The London Train Bands were to be the backbone of the Roundhead infantry, as Cromwell's Ironsides would be of the cavalry.

HANSON, EDWIN 1886 *Merchant Taylor.* Five thousand people crammed into Guildhall to celebrate Queen Victoria's Golden Jubilee in 1887. The Kings of Denmark, Belgium, Greece and Saxony headed the guests list which included almost the entire Royal Family numbering several score, close kin of the monarchs of Russia, Germany and Austria, ambassadors, bishops, peers and a colourful sprinkling of Indian princes whose jewels would have paid off the national debt.

Hanson had done his best, but the Queen Empress was also the Widow of Windsor, and her mourning robes reminded everyone how empty was such a celebration without dear Albert, and how little comfort she found in the presence of the portly Prince of Wales.

'Wider still and wider' spread the boundaries of an Empire on which the sun never set, and no potentate calling on the Queen Empress failed to pay a call on the Lord Mayor. Among the more eye-catching were the Sultan of Turkey, the Khedive of Egypt, the Shah of Persia and Tsar Alexander.

HARDEL, RALPH 1254-57 *guild unknown.* Henry III enjoyed a brief popularity when the French king sent him an elephant, the first seen in Britain since the arrival of several from Rome for the Triumph of Claudius in 43 AD.

Mayor Hardel did it proud with a covered cage, but the elephant pined for sunny Africa and died. The king was incensed when he

Buried in Tower ditch (Elephant)

heard it had been buried in the Tower ditch, and had its bones disinterred and removed to the Abbey.

The German Emperor's gift proved more hardy and his three leopards, a neat compliment on Royal Coat of Arms, formed the nucleus of the Royal Collection in the Lion Tower. This menagerie, open to all, was the prime tourist attraction of the Middle Ages, and beside the leopards there were a couple of lions, monkeys, a hyena, the ravens, an eagle, an ostrich and always a bear or two.

Not until the 1830s were the Royal Menageries at the Tower and Windsor Castle moved to the new Zoological Gardens in Regent's Park.

HARVEY, SEBASTIAN 1618 *Ironmonger.* James I selected 29th October, the day of the Lord Mayor's Show, for the execution of Sir Walter Raleigh. He hoped that 'pageants and fine shows might draw away the people from beholding the tragedy of one of the gallantest worthies that ever England bred'.

James miscalculated, and it was Mayor Harvey who went on his way through empty streets while the Londoners thronged Tower Hill to watch the last of the great Elizabethans go to his death to placate Spain and the King's shameful expediency transformed one country MP into an implacable enemy of the Stuarts from that day onwards. He witnessed the 'guards and officers about him, the scaffold and the executioner, the axe and the more cruel expectation of his enemies'. But Raleigh did not flinch, dying as gallantly as he had lived before an admiring crowd.

As for Mayor Harvey his great day was ruined. He went on his way through empty streets, and to the distant cheers of his fellow citizens saluting a hero who knew how to die as gallantly as he had lived.

Sir Walter Rayleigh

HEATHCOTE, GILBERT 1710 *Vintner.* Lavish expenditure on three Lord Mayors within ten years was too much to expect of Company funds. The Vintners were constrained to cut back on a display to equal Dashwood's 1702 Triumph, but Heathcote was allotted an escort of drummers and trumpeters when he set out for Westminster. The cacophony was too much for his horse which reared and threw him, causing no injury to his person but immense damage to his pride. From then on Lord Mayors have relied on the safety and dignity of a coach.

There must have been many in the crowd who cheered to see the Lord Mayor humbled, for Heathcote was not well liked. He was the second Governor of the Bank of England, and had called out a troop of Horse Guards to subdue a mob threatening to break into the Bank after a sensational trial had led to the jailing of a popular preacher. He was the City's MP and reputed to be a many-acred land owner, the richest commoner in the land and a stern man of business with no sympathy for those who fell upon hard times. Alexander Pope sneered that: *The grave Sir Gilbert holds it for a rule*
That every man in want is knave or fool.

HEWET, WILLIAM 1559 *Clothworker.* One of the City's favourite tales is of the apprentice falling in love with the Lord Mayor's daughter.

Hewet had a house on London Bridge, some windows overlooking the narrow street and others hanging out over the water. Somehow his only child scrambled out of a window and fell into the Thames. Luckily his apprentice, Edward Osborne, leaped into the river and dragged the little girl to safety. Anne grew into a beautiful and much-courted heiress, but old Mayor Hewet sent all her suitors packing with the words 'Osborne saved her, Osborne shall have her', and so he did. He also inherited the business and in 1583 became Lord Mayor in his turn, and his descendants, whose family name is still Osborne, rose to be the Dukes of Leeds.

HOUBLON, JOHN 1695 *Grocer.* The Houblons were Huguenot refugees, and John was one of several brothers to make their mark in the London of William and Mary. He was the first Governor of the Bank of England, founded in 1694 to finance the French war, and was later a Lord of the Admiralty. The first meetings were held in Mercers' Hall but shortly moved to Grocer's Hall, where they remained for the next four decades.

All Europe was at war with Louis XIV, and soon the Bank had agents in Amsterdam, Hamburg, Madrid, Lisbon, Venice and Genoa, and one of its major tasks was to act as paymaster to the British army in Flanders. Houblon's deputy Governor, Michael Godfrey , was killed when delivering a chest of gold coins to William III when the King was visiting his troops in Flanders.

Houblon died in 1711, but only after his widow's death was his house in Threadneedle Street and St Bartholomew by the Exchange pulled down to make room for Soane's 'Money Box', the new Bank of England.

HUMPHREYS, WILLIAM 1714 *Ironmonger.* 'Queen Anne is dead'! She was the last of the Stuarts, and when she died the succession passed sideways and backwards, to the son of a fifth daughter of the only

Osborne's heroic leap

daughter of James I.

The new king always felt himself firstly Elector of Hanover and never bothered to learn English, but he did comply with tradition by dining at Guildhall on Lord Mayor's Day. Humphreys was given a baronetcy, other aldermen came away with knighthoods and the burden of poor debtors was lightened by the King's gift of £1000.

Had the First Jacobite Rising, the '15', in support of the Old Pretender swept Scotland and then threatened London, Mayor Humphreys would have taken command of the Train Bands and put the City in a 'posture of defence'.

It was the Old Pretender's son, Bonnie Prince Charlie, who was to cause panic in London in December 1745 when his army reached the Midlands. This rising seriously threatened the capital and the King made plans to flee to Hanover and Mayor Richard Hoare called on the Honourable Artillery Company and the Militia to stand to their arms.

Ironmongers

Miscellany of Mayors

JUDDE – the much travelled benefactor
KEBLE – gave £200 for poor maids' dowries
KENNET – read the Riot Act too late
KEYSER – failed to catch Jack the Ripper
LARGE – the Mercer who took Caxton as an apprentice

Skinner

JAMES, BARTHOLOMEW 1479 *Draper.*
Pestilence had always stalked the streets of London and anyone who coughed or sneezed was a suspected Plague carrier. Mayor James was taking no chances, and not only distanced himself from his Sheriff in St Paul's, but fined him fifty marks for kneeling too close.

JUDDE, ANDREW 1550 *Skinner.* Judde was a Tudor merchant prince whose wealth and benefactions equalled Thomas Gresham's. He was Mayor in the brief reign of Edward VI, five times Master of the Skinners, Surveyor General of Hospitals and Treasurer of Barts.

Judde founded a Grammar School at Tonbridge in his native Kent and the annual founder's day is known as Skinners Day. It adopted Judde's motto *Deus dat Incrementum* – 'God gives the Increase', though modern parents are apt to mutter 'but its the Skinners who put up the fees'.

Judde is buried in St Helen's Bishopsgate, and appears as one of the 'Ten Worthies' in the west window. His cosmopolitan career took him to:

Russia and Mussova, to Spayne, Gynny withoute fable
traveled he by land and sea.
Bothe mayre of London and Staple, the Commonwealth he nourished
So worthelie in all his daies that ech state full well him loved

to his perpetuall prayes'.
Three wyves he had, one was Mary,
Fower sunes one mayde he had by her,
Annys had none by him truly,
By Dame Margaret had one dowghtier'
Judde was a great-grandson of Robert Chichele, Mayor in 1411

Tonbridge Scholl Arms of Judde

Gordon Riots

KEBLE, HENRY 1510 *Grocer.* During his lifetime he paid for the rebuilding of St Mary Aldermary and his epitaph named him a 'famous Wight, who was sometime of London Maior, which did this Aldermary Church erect and set upright. Here he sate, of Grocers worthy Companie, the chiefest in his state which in this City grew to Wealth and unto worship came'. More enduring than his tomb were bequests of £200 for the upkeep of the highways, £200 for poor maids' dowries, and the practical gift of 140 ploughshares for farmers in Warwick and Oxfordshire.

Tudor London overflowed with the living, and the churches with the dead, and in 1556 Keble's bones were 'unkindly cast out and his Monument pulled downe' to make way for Mayors William Laxton, 1544, founder of Oundle School, and Thomas Lodge, 1562.

KENNET, BRACKLEY 1779 *Vintner* He had the misfortune to hold office during the Gordon Riots, public disorders sparked off when the government tried to ease the penal laws against Catholics. Two hundred years after the Armada agitators and demagogues could still whip up the Londoners with cries of 'no Popery'.

Lord George Gordon was a deranged but popular orator, and 50,000 of 'the better sort of tradesmen in their sabbath day cloathes' followed him to Parliament with a gigantic Protestant Petition which the government unwisely ignored. The enraged crowd turned into a mob, and the rioting that followed came close to what would soon be unleashed in revolutionary Paris.

The chapels and houses of Catholic ambassadors and English co- religionists were looted and burned and then the Fleet and Newgate jails were stormed. Swollen by the released prisoners the mob swept on to attack the Bank of England.

Belatedly Mayor Kennet read the Riot Act, and John Wilkes with the London Military Association repulsed the crowd at the Royal Exchange. Baulked of gold the mob ransacked Langdale's Brewery and soon 120,000 gallons of gin were pouring into the gutters. As a Vintner the Mayor must have been appalled at the waste, and Dickens later set 'Barnaby Rudge'against a background of the Gordon Riots.

Mayor Kennet was blamed for 'querelous ineptitude' and delay in calling out the troops, while Wilkes lost the mob's favour for siding with the authorities. Lord George Gordon spent the rest of his demented life in rebuilt Newgate. A convert to Judaism he called himself Israel bar Abraham Gordon, wrote scurrilous letters to the Pope, played the bagpipes and died of jail fever in 1793.

KEYSER, POLYDORE de 1887 *Spectacle-maker*. A Belgian by birth he built the Keyser Hotel on the Embankment, now the site of Unilever House.

A shadowy murderer, soon labelled Jack the Ripper, terrorised East End prostitutes in the autumn of 1888. The fourth killing took place in the City after the drunk and disorderly Catharine Eddowes had been released from Bishopsgate Police Station in the early hours of 1st October. She returned to her beat, but in the morning her mutilated body was found in Mitre Square. The Lord Mayor was urged to intensify the hunt for the killer, but was as baffled by the crimes as the Home Secretary and Commissioner of Police.

The last killing was on 9th November, the day of de Keyser's successor's Show, James Whitehead. Two suspects later committed suicide, but the Ripper's true identity has never been proved — was he a qualified doctor, a wellknown barrister or a psychopathic member of the Royal Family?

LAMBARDE, NICHOLAS 1531. *Grocer*. Not all festivities took place in Guildhall, and one at Ely Place in May 1530 must have satisfied even Henry VIII.

The feast lasted for five days and among those entertained were the King and Katharine of Aragon, the Lord Mayor, ambassadors, judges, barons of the Exchequer, aldermen and courtiers. The ladies were entertained in a separate chamber. The meat came from the slaughterhouses of Smithfield and the clerk of the bishop's kitchens supervised the preparation of: 24 great beefs, one carcass of an ox, 100 fat muttons, 51 veals, 34 porks, 91 pigges, 19 dozen capons, 14 dozen cocks, 37 dozen pigeons, 14 dozen swans and 340 dozen larks.

LANE, THOMAS 1694 *Clothworker*. The Company made great use of its barge during the summer months and one day 'took their Ladies as high as Putney and then returned to dine at Chelsea to see the College and the Physic Garden'.

Mayor Lane was seen off to Westminster in the barge to a peal of Ordnance, and on his return to the water stairs at Baynard's Castle was met by more gunfire from the Honourable Artillery Company who escorted him through the streets with 'Drums, Fifes, Trumpets, Colours, Silkwork, Pensioners, Gentlemen Ushers, Budge Bachelors and Foynes Bachelors'.

For a fee of £10 the poet and impresario, Elkanah Settle, wrote a quartet of orations for Lane's Show, and the Company was not shortchanged. Jason, Augusta, Virtue, Piety, Apollo, Concord and Jsutice rubbed shoulders with Asia, Africa, America, the Thames, Tiber, Nile and Indus all 'intimating to the whole World the Wealth and Grandeur of London ... applied to My Lord (Mayor) as being the Representative of Majesty within the City of London'.

Speeches were declaimed from the 'Seat of Sovereignty, the Garden of Plenty, the Chariot of Apollo and the Pageant of Truth'. The theme of the Show being the grandeur of the City and glory of the Clothworkers, much play was made with the 'Gold of our Fleece and the Wealth of our Loom' being in a manner 'our whole English Peru'.

LARGE, ROBERT 1439 *Mercer*. In his will Large gave 40 marks for a new water conduit and 200 marks towards covering in the stinking river Walbrook near St Margaret's Lothbury.

In the introduction to the first book ever printed in Britain Caxton states 'I was born and lerned myn englissh in Kente in the Weeld, where I doubte not is spoken as brode and rude englissh as in ony part of englond'. He was apprenticed to Robert Large, and lived with the Mercer's family in Old Jewry close to Guildhall. Apprentices at this time were treated more like favoured pupils than the exploited youngsters of Dickens' day, and Caxton's father would have paid a high premium to this fellow Mercer to indenture his son.

When one of their own was elected Mayor the Mercers spared no expense, and they paid out £5.6.8 for sixteen trumpeters in new tabards to escort Large to Westminster, and any members who stayed away were heavily fined. As a Mercer William Caxton was among four fined in 1453 for absenting themselves from Mayor John Norman's procession.

LAWRENCE, JOHN 1664 *Haberdasher*. By his steadfast example Lawrence induced many in authority to stay at their posts during the Plague, and he issued special preventive Plague Orders from Guildhall. Watch was to be set on the City gates to keep out those infected, suspected houses should be locked up, public entertainments forbidden, taverns closed, cats and dogs rounded up and killed and vermin where found exterminated. Had there been the manpower to carry out the Orders they might have been effective, but by the time they came into force the Pestilence was not to be stopped and the victims listed in the Bills of Mortality reached a peak in September 1665.

Brave Sir John, whose Show in torrential rain had been adjudged a 'most magnificent triumph by Water and Land', must have found some comfort at home during these dreadful months. The tomb of his wife, Dame Abigail Lawrence, extols her as a 'tender mother of ten children, the nine first being all daughters. She was an exemplary matron of this Cittie'.

Caxton's Sign

LEIGH, THOMAS 1558 *Mercer*. Two months after her accession Queen Elizabeth made a triumphal entry into London in January 1559. A pictorial record made by the College of Heralds and shows the Queen in a horsedrawn litter escorted by her Favourite, Lord Robert Dudley, his brother Ambrose and Lord Giles Paulet. In the centre of the procession rides the 'Lord Maior', bareheaded and wearing a tabard, between the Duke of Norfolk, Earl Marshall of England, and Garter King of Arms.

A Victory Service at St Paul's in November 1588 celebrated the Defeat of the Spanish Armada, 'when God blew and they were scattered'. Here Mayor Martin Calthorp is in the familiar company of the Earl Marshall and Garter King of Arms, but this time he rides ahead of the French ambassador.

LOWSON, DENYS 1950 *Grocer*. Air Marshall Lord Trenchard proudly replied to a request by the American Air Force to build a shrine to their war dead, that 'it is not for you, but for us to erect that memorial'.

On Fourth July 1951 a service of remembrance was held in St Paul's attended by the royal family, representatives of the American government and services and the Mayor and Corporation. The Roll of Honor of 28,000 names was presented by General Eisenhower.

In the mayoralty of Harold Gillett in 1958 a further service was held to dedicate the finished American Chapel behind the high altar of St Paul's. Nixon when Vice-President was there, and the Queen unveiled a tablet in the marble floor − 'To the American Dead of the Second World War from the people of Britain'.

LUCAS, MATTHIAS PRIME 1827 *Vintner*. New lighting had been installed in Guildhall for Lucas' Mayoral Banquet, but it all came crashing down on the top table showering the distinguished guests with hot oil and lamp black. A cartoonist mocked this undignified 'Civic Annointing' with a sketch of the cowering Mayor Lucas and his Lady pleading with the Duke of Wellington to cut away the flaming debris with his sword, while Gog and Magog exchange knowing winks.

Miscellany of Mayors

M-P

Draper

MERCER – ranked with the barons at Runnymede
NEWSON-SMITH – made do with a frugal wartime feast at 5/- a head
PENNINGTON – sent housewives' Sunday dinners to Civil War troops
PHILPOT – the battling Grocer whose fleet beat the pirates
PICARD – turned a blind eye to a king cheating at cards

MALORYE, RICHARD 1564 *Mercer*. At a Lenten service in St Paul's the Queen took offence at the sermon, and Malorye stood by while she harangued the preacher.

Elizabeth had no time for fanatics, and when the rabid protestant cleric thundered against popish idolatry Her Majesty shouted back, 'to your text, Master Dean, to your text, we have heard enough'.

She felt affection for her mother's old chaplain Matthew Parker, but she could not stomach a married priest, particularly an Archbishop of Canterbury. After dining at Lambeth Palace she addressed Parker's lady coldly, 'Madam, I may not, Mistress, I am ashamed to call you, but I thank you for your hospitality'.

The Virgin Queen may not have warmed to the Lady Mayoress either, since Malorye's wife was the mother of 19 children.

MATHEWE, JOHN 1490 *Mercer*. Mathewe was one of very few bachelor Mayors, and most of his successors followed the practical advice of a Tudor commentator that 'a lady Mayoress is something more than ornamental to a Lord Mayor, their wives' great portions or good providence much advantaging their estates to be capable of so high a dignity'.

MERCER, SERLO le 1215 *Mercer*. The first three Mayors were all Mercers, and Serlo received the second City charter from the reluctant hands of King John in May 1215. The four previous City charters dating back to 1067 were reconfirmed, and the important new right granted 'to choose every year a Mayor'.

In June Serlo joined the 24 barons at Runnymede who forced the King to set his seal to *Magna Carta*, the Great Charter that is hallowed for all time as enshrining the rights of the common people against the arbitrary rule of the monarch. What it amounted to at the time was a blueprint for a few over-mighty subjects to curtail the unbridled power of a medieval warlord, but through the centuries its high-sounding provisions that 'to none will we deny or delay, right or justice' did extend to cover all citizens.

MOORE, JOHN 1898 *Loriner*. Volunteers rushed to the Colours when the Boer War broke out and flags were unfurled and the national anthem sung on the floor of the Stock Exchange. A thousand stockbrokers then converged on Guildhall and handed over £22,000 to the Lord Mayor's Fund for Transvaal Refugees

The Mayor personally enrolled 1,500 young men into the newly- formed City Imperial Volunteers, the CIVs, and bestowed the Freedom of the city on each recruit before handing over a £25,000 grant to equip the new regiment.

MUSGROVE, JOHN 1850 *Clothworker*. The Clothworkers' barge had mouldered away long before Musgrove went by river to Westminster, and he had to make do with a borrowed craft, javelins on loan from the Goldsmiths and a band of freelance musicians.

The Great Exhibition of 1851 had been partially sponsored by the City Companies, reluctantly accepting the Royal Invitation to become promoters. It proved a global triumph, and grateful for the boost to trade the City invited the Queen and Prince Albert to a memorable banquet.

The austere vaulted crypt of Guildhall was transformed into a gothic castle replete with reproduction baronial coffers and oak settles. These were reflected in gilded mirrors and alcoves and niches loaded down with civic and Company gold plate and parcel gilt. Sweating policeman stood motionless against a replica of the Bayeux Tapestry,

each man clad in full armour loaned out by the Tower. Only a tartan carpet was missing, but Albert the Good was said to have been greatly impressed.

Musgrove was an auctioneer, and it was probably a case of 'what am I bid' for these gothick souvenirs after the event.

NASH, WILLIAM 1771 *Salter*. The Mayor was 'roughly used by the populace for not lowering the price of bread'. Food riots had erupted since the Middle Ages with bad harvests, impassable roads, war and epidemics all affecting supplies to the ever-expanding capital. Staple foods were still bread, meat and beer, and in consultation with the Baker's Company an Assize of Bread fixing the price of a loaf was issued weekly from Guildhall.

An early *Assisa Panis* of the Bakers had 19 clauses with price variations allowed due to the costs of grain, labour and fuel; Brown Bakers and White Bakers must not make other bread; every baker to set his mark on each loaf and no 'forestalling' the market by buying up corn before nine in the morning. For fear of accusations of giving shortweight bakers often threw in an extra vantage loaf, giving 13 for the price of 12 to make up the

Crystal Palace, partially sponsored by the City Companies

'baker's dozen'. In 1746 a penny loaf weighed 8 ounces.

The rate was set for a 'penny loaf', since it was weight not price that was variable. In 1815 did Parliament took over bread pricing when, in a reversal of the old practice, the *weight* of the 'standard loaf' was fixed and the *price* left to market forces.

NEWSON-SMITH, JOHN 1943 *Turner*. In 1909 when the City of London Solicitors' Company was formed it was the first new Company since the Fanmakers in 1709.

Letters Patent were not presented until May 1944, when Mayor Newson-Smith entertained the Master and Company at the Mansion House. Wartime food regulations meant a 5/- meal which hardly did justice to the Egyptian Hall: mock turtle soup, roast chicken and trifle, only made palatable by a '34 Macon and an '08 Crofts port.

The 250th anniversary of the Bank of England also fell in 1944, and among the guests of the Lord Mayor at another frugal meal were the Chancellor and the Masters of the Mercers and the Grocers, whose Halls had served as the Bank's first premises. Few present could compare these meagre repasts with the Solicitors' Inaugural Dinner in January 1909 attended by Mayor George Truscott. This started with *genuine* turtle or turtle soup, and after courses of turbot, whitebait, foie gras, saddle of mutton, pheasant, ham, jellies, souffles and gateaux ended with mysterious 'croutes a la Bismarck'. The list of wines was almost as long as that of the speechmakers: punch, sherry, Moselle, claret, two champagnes, port and liquers.

NORMAN, JOHN 1453 *Draper*. Being lame Norman had difficulty mounting a horse, so went to Westminster along the Thames in a magnificent barge 'sumptuously furnished' at his own charge with banners and gilded oars. Other Company barges were in the flotilla all 'well decked and trimmed to pass along with him', and from these comes the term 'float'.

The River Pageant continued for centuries, and was immensely popular and profitable with the Thames watermen, who long remembered their benefactor in the song 'Row thy boat, Norman, to thy leman'. (leman — lady love)

NORTHAMPTON, JOHN de 1381-82 *Draper*. Elected in the October following the Peasants' Revolt which he had helped to put down with Walworth and Brembre. Northampton's patron was John of Gaunt, whose sacked Savoy Palace in the Strand was rebuilt during his mayoralty. Edward III had died in 1377, having sired seven sons, but his heir the Black Prince predeceased him. Richard II was the Prince's 11 year-old son, and though the Wars of the Roses were still fifty years off, the seeds were already germinating.

Northampton headed the craft Companies led by his own Drapers and the Mercers, who were permanently disputing with the victualling Companies of the Bakers, Butchers, Brewers, and above all Fishmongers. Cheap food was always the issue, and the obligatory fish days put monopolistic power into the hands of the fish merchants. The Mayor ordered bread and beer to be sold by the farthing's worth, and had a man pilloried with rotten herrings round his neck for selling stale fish. He so hated the Fishmongers that he forced through an Act of Common Council that 'no Fishmonger could become Mayor', but this was soon overturned and Nicholas Exton, aldermen for Billingsgate, became Mayor in 1386.

PARSONS, JOHN 1703 *Brewer — Fishmonger*. Blenheim was the first of Marlboroughs triumphs over the French in August 1704, and it was celebrated with the 'utmost pompe and splendour by the Court, greate officers, Lord Mayor and Sheriffs'. The streets were hung with tapestries around Temple Bar where Mayor Parsons presented the City's sword to Queen Anne to touch on her way to St Paul's, and the Militia were out in force with every Company ranged under its banners with trumpeters.

The Mayor and Aldermen rode brightly bedecked horses ahead of the Royal Coach carrying the bejewelled Queen and her dearest friend, the Duchess of Marlborough. After the service the Nobility and bishops were entertained at various livery Halls and the cheering crowds did not go to bed until the last firework spluttered out in the Thames.

Two years later another military pageant greeted the victor of Ramillies when Marlborough and his Duchess were welcomed to the City by Mayor Thomas Rawlinson. 26 captured French standards and 63 regimental colours were paraded through the streets and then put on display as trophies of war in Guildhall.

PECKHAM, ROBERT 1783 *Wheelwright.*
Since Robert Willimot had refused to 'translate' to one of the Great Twelve in 1742 most members remained with their original Companies, and Peckham was the first Wheelwright Lord Mayor.

'Translation' was still possible, but it was neither a tactful nor a cheap option. In 1803 a new Sheriff moving to the Fishmongers had to pay the Wheelwright's a fee of £200 for abandoning them.

For Peckham's Swearing-In the Company all Wheelwrights were commanded to attend at Westminster, and new standards and Livery robes were ordered for his Show. The banners were magnificent being 'emblazon with the Arms of England, the Arms of the City, the Arms of the Company, two yards square, each of Rich Mantua silk fringed round with silk fringe with Poles and twined trunks Gilt. Compleat for the sum of £38.13.'.

England was at war with France, and the Wheelwrights deemed it patriotic to cut back on feasting and instead pay '£100 into the Bank for the Defence of the Country against Invasion'. Many accounts for their wining and dining still exist and the caterer's bill for Lord Mayor's Day 1779 cost them £12.11s for wine, punch and brandy, £2.10s for tea and coffee and 10/- for strong beer. They were also charged 21/- for tips and 5/- for the 'glass broke'.

PECOCKE, STEPHEN 1532 *Haberdasher.*
The marriage of Anne Boleyn to Henry VIII was a private affair, but her coronation on lst June 1533 was a state occasion. During the endless haggling over the Divorce the Londoners had been staunchly for Katharine of Aragon, but they were prepared to enjoy the festivities of someone whose great-grandfather had been Lord Mayor and a Mercer — Geoffrey Boleyn/Bullen in 1457.

Their Majesties were at Greenwich, and Pecocke in a gorgeously appointed barge led the Companies vessels downstream to escort them to the state apartments in the Tower. Anne's barge was hung with silk and velvet, and tinkled with the silver bells of a tethered white falcon in the stern. Her dark beauty was set off by a starburst of precious stones, but it must have rankled that these were new trinkets. Katharine, daughter of Their Most Catholic Majesties, had refused to hand over the royal jewels 'to adorn a person the scandal of Christendom and the King's disgrace'.

Next day, escorted again by Mayor Pecocke and the aldermen, the procession passed through the City to Westminster Hall, greeted at selected spots by pageants, tableaux and choirs of children while the conduits ran with wine. Anne defiantly wore her hair unbound as a virgin bride, but she rode in a horsedrawn litter for there was no disguising that 'her condition doth well appear as being somewhat big with child'.

PENNINGTON, ISAAC 1642 *Fishmonger.*
When Gurney was ousted at the start of the Civil War Alderman Pennington, Colonel in the White Regiment of the Train Bands, stepped in as Lord Mayor.

After Edgehill the Train Bands were pursued by Prince Rupert and his cavalry, and dug in for a last ditch stand at Turnham Green. Pennington ordered the City preachers to call on the housewives to bring their Sunday dinners to Guildhall which were then carted westwards to sustain the troops. Rupert had scoffed at the City regiments of 'butchers and dyers', but despite heavy losses they repulsed him, and never again did the Royalist army come so close to taking the capital.

The Common Council petitioned King Charles to return to London and negotiate, but his reply was uncompromising: 'what hope His Majesty can have for safety there whilst Alderman Pennington, their pretended Lord Mayor, the principal author of these calamities which so neerly threaten the ruine of that famous City ... commit such outrages'. After the King's death Pennington served as one of Cromwell's Councillor's of State.

PERRING, JOHN 1703 *Clothworker*. 'The greatest storme that was ever in England' struck on 27th November 1703 and lasted nine hours. Hundreds were killed and in London 'all ships in the river were driven ashore, barges were driven against the arches of London Bridge and smashed into splinters and four hundred of the watermen's wherries were sunk or broken'. Two thousand chimneys were blown down, spires and pinnacles of churches crashed to the ground, many trees were uprooted and the lead on the roofs of the highest buildings was rolled up like paper.

Mayor Perring called for government aid for the stricken capital while Christopher Wren viewed the devastation with a certain satisfaction. None of his new churches had been badly damaged, and the flying buttresses and slender spire of St Dunstan in the East, which critics had derided as unsafe, had survived unscathed. The Blitzed church is now a garden but the spire still soars above the City, as the pre-Fire steeple does in the prints of Fisscher and Hollar.

Only the very old in Perring's day could recall the tempest that had raged the night Cromwell died in September 1658, and these two storms were not to be equalled in ferocity until the Hurricane struck southern England in October 1987.

PHILPOT, JOHN 1378 *Grocer*. The Mayor had jurisdiction over the Thames, but early in the reign of Edward II the new Admiral of the Port of London took his role more seriously than most and fitted out a fleet at his own expense. Barbary pirates from the Moslem shores of North Africa infested the waters around Britain from the Channel to the North Sea, and their swift raids on unprotected settlements swept them clean of all manpower to replenish the chained oarsmen in the galleys. Many contemporary Christian wills have bequests to 'ransom poor Englyshmen from ye Infidels' or to 'free from captivitie trueborn subjects of the Kynge from the heathen Turkes'.

Philpot's ships, crewed by a thousand tough London watermen, won a famous battle off the coast of Yorkshire and arrived back in the capital laden with loot. They had

Goldsmiths

also picked up as prizes fifteen unlucky Spanish ships which had strayed into the fight.

Mayor Philpot then redeemed the weapons and armour of the King's guard from pawn, and lent his fleet for the Hundred Years War. Once more an alderman, he helped restore order after the Peasants' Revolt and was given a long overdue knighthood. Philpot Lane off Eastcheap is named after the battling grocer.

PICARD, HENRY 1356 *Vintner*. The City fathers were a close knit group, bound together by ties of trade and marriage, and Picard's wife was the heiress daughter of John de Gisors, Mayor in 1311. The next Mayor was John Stodeye, his brother-in-law, and his four daughters spread the net of wedlock further, two of them marrying future Mayors, Idonia to Nicholas Brembre, 1383, and Margaret to John Philpot, 1378.

An enduring legend credits Picard with entertaining five monarchs to a great feast in his mansion in Vintry. They were Edward III of England, David of Scotland, John of France and the kings of Denmark and Cyprus. After the banquet they took to gambling at dice and hazard, but the King of Cyprus, Peter de Lusignan, being a bad loser jibbed at paying his debts to a mere commoner. The Mayor gallantly begged 'be not aggrieved, I covet not your gold but your play, for I have not bidden you hither that you might grieve you but that amongst other things I might try your play', and returned his wager together with several rich gifts.

Modern historians object that all five kings were never in London together, but a 14th century chronicle asserts that 'such a thing had never been seen since the time of King Arthur, for whose feast at Caerleon six kings were present'. The toast of 'prosperity to the Vintners Company' is always accompanied by five cheers in honour of Picard's and the kings. The Vintners never do things by twos and threes, and Mayor Truscott came close to rivalling Picard in 1880 when he entertained four princes, all sons of Queen Victoria.

PULTENEY, JOHN de 1330/31/33/36 *Draper* Military adventures were always ruinously expensive, and de Pulteney lent vast sums to Edward III during the early years of the Hundred Years War. The King visited him at his Thameside mansion of Cold Harbour where the draper carried on business close to the landing stage of Old Swan Stairs.

He also had a country estate at Penshurst in Kent which passed eventually to the Sidney family, who later had the coveted but costly honour of entertaining Elizabeth on a Royal Progress. Cold Harbour was pulled down after Pulteney's time, but Wren's St Nicholas Cole Abbey stands close to the site.

A ship typical of Mayor Philpot's Fleet

Miscellany of Mayors

Cutlers

SHAA – did he share his wife with Edward IV?
SALOMONS – the first Jewish Lord Mayor
STARLING – promised a fortune and paid out
half a crown
TRECOTHICK – damned as a traitor for backing the American Colonists

REST, JOHN 1516 *Grocer*. Aliens were commonplace in Tudor London but always suspect, and on 1st May 1517, Evil May Day, this distrust and dislike spilled over into bloodshed. Rowdy apprentices broke the windows of foreign merchants and bankers and roughed-up any Spaniards, Germans or Flemings who crossed their path. The City Fathers panicked, first ordering the Lieutenant of the Tower to prime his cannon, and then sending word of the disorder to the King.

The affray had fizzled out by next morning and the lads were back at work, but Henry V111 was determined to make a ferocious example of the ringleaders. A special court found them guilty of treason and thirteen 'poor younglings' were hanged. Dozens more were paraded with halters round their necks and only the combined pleas of Queen Katharine, Thomas More and Mayor Rest eventually led to their pardon.

The City had been given an awesome foretaste of the King's supreme power, and the Venetian envoy's despatch that 'the terror has been greater than the harm' was all too accurate.

ROBINSON, JOHN 1662 *Clothworker*. Threatened rioting in the City kept the royal family away from Robinson's Show and Feast, to the regret of the Portuguese Queen who had never witnessed the spectacle.

His pageant celebrated 'London's Triumph at the Charge of the Clothworkers Company' and the Royal balcony in Cheapside was occupied only by a Danish prince and a few maids of honour. John Evelyn watched from the house next door, and within the month dined privately with Mayor Robinson and the Lieutenant of the Tower.

RYDER, WILLIAM 1600 *Haberdasher*. Mayor Ryder and several aldermen watched with anxious eyes, and lightened wallets, as a small fleet of merchant ships sailed from Woolwich in February 1601. It was the first venture of the East India Company, a fledgling group that had received a charter from the ageing Elizabeth on the last day of the old century.

Its aim was to break the monopoly of the Portuguese and the Dutch on the fabled riches of the East Indies and the Spice Islands, and it succeeded beyond the dreams of avarice. By early 18th century this highly speculative project had blossomed into the great 'John Company', the virtual master of the sub-continent and precursor of the Indian Civil Service.

SALOMONS, DAVID 1855 *Cooper*. Catholics were banned from public office from the Reformation until shortly before the Great Reform Bill, roughly 1530s – 1820s, and for those three centuries any cry of 'No Popery' conjured up a mob. One of the '39 Articles' of the Anglican Church still claims that 'the Bishop of Rome has no jurisdiction in this realm of England'.

By 1700 few believed a foreign power dominated the catholic Faithful, but it was political suicide to say so, and the ban on holding public office included Dissenters and Jews.

Salomons was London's first Jewish Lord Mayor, although it had caused a problem when as Sheriff he refused to take the oath in its traditional form. Two years after his Mayoralty, Lionel de Rothschild, one of the 18th century Frankfurt banking dynasty, entered the Commons as the City MP, and this trio of firsts was rounded off in 1868 by Prime Minister Benjamin Disraeli.

SALTONSTALL, RICHARD 1597 *Skinner.* In Armada year Saltonstall was an MP and a Sheriff, but he got a flea in the ear from the Queen for offering unwanted advice to the Navy during his year of office a decade later. He was commanded 'not to intermeddle with any causes relating to maritime affairs but to refer the same to the Lord Admiral'.

In the summer of 1588 he was living in Essex close to Tilbury Fort, and when not attending at Guildhall or Westminster he was busy as a merchant adventurer trading with the Low Countries. These links brought him to the notice of Lord Treasurer Burleigh, and Saltonstall may have negotiated war loans on the Antwerp Exchange.

He lived to be eighty, fathered fifteen children, invested in the early East India Company and, despite the regal ticking-off, was knighted by Elizabeth in his Mayoral year.

SANDWICH, RALPH de 1285-1292 *guild unknown.* Edward III had already suspended the Mayoralty, and when he banished all Jews from the kingdom in 1290 it was de Sandwich as Warden who ejected them from the ghetto in Old Jewry.

To Christians moneylending was usury, so it was the Jews who lent money to kings, mayors and aldermen, which was seldom repaid in full. They were segregated and abused, and Aaron of London and other Jews were fined over 20,000 marks in one

Royal Standard

Queen Elizabeth I

year alone. Their houses were seen as handy quarries and often demolished to rebuild the City walls. When Ludgate was repaired in Armada year a stone was found inscribed 'this is the house of Rabbi Moses, son of Rabbi Isaac'.

SEVENOKE, WILLIAM 1418, *Grocer.*
Another simple, country boy to make good
in London. His Mayoral coat of arms bore
seven acorns, either to commemorate his
birthplace or the rumour that he had been a
foundling discovered in a hollow oak tree
and adopted by a Master Rumschedde. He
was knighted by Henry V, and Whittington
followed him for his fourth term as Mayor.

Sevenoke was the first Mayor to endow a
school in his native town, and when it Seven-
oaks School opened in 1432 it was one of
only eleven such establishments in England.
It was fortunate it took the name of his town
rather than his adoptive father or old boys
would be known as Rumscheddeans, not
Sennockians.

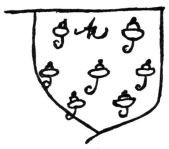

Shield of Sevenoaks

SHAA, EDMUND 1482 *Goldsmith* Shaa,
Shaw, Shoor, Shore? People spelled their
names as the fancy took them, and Shakespeare seldom signed his name twice in the
same way, 'Shaxberd' was one variation. Legend has it that Jane Shore, 'the Goldsmith's
wife' and mistress of Edward IV might have
been the Lady Mayoress.

The 'corpulent and burly king' was irresist-
ible to the ladies, and his own wife Elizabeth,
she of the silver-gilt hair, ignored his amo-
rous conquests so long as no-one threatened
her hold on the crown. Jane was more than a
buxom armful, and King and Mayor were
lucky to share one who had 'a proper wit,
could read and write and was merry in company, being neither mute nor full of babble'.

SHAA, JOHN 1501 *Goldsmith.* Shaa's banquet set the precedent for all future feasts,
and was served from kitchens newly installed
in Guildhall. Today over 600 can sit down to
dine in the Hall, but the advent of the deep
freeze and microwave oven has seen the
kitchens converted into mere serveries.

The 'ladye princesse of Spayne', Katharine
of Aragon, was welcomed by Mayor Shaa
heading a goodly pageant on her arrival in
London. The procession halted six times before reaching St Paul's so tableaux could be
enacted before the Infanta. The first on London Bridge had a 'fair ladye with a wheel in
her hand in a likenesse of St Catharine', and
the other five were at Gracechurch Street,
the Conduit in Cornhill, the Conduit in

Edward IV

Cheap, the Standard in Cheap and at Paul's
Cross. The long day was rounded off with a
banquet.

The Venetian envoy wrote home that
'within London the Mayor is next unto the
King in all manner of things, and no-one can
be mayor or alderman who has not been an
apprentice in his youth, who has not passed
the seven or nine years in that hard service

... of these twenty four aldermen one is elected every year by themselves, to be a magistrate named the Mayor, who is in no less estimation with the Londoners than the person of our most serene lord, the Doge, is with us. The Day on which he enters office he is obliged to give a sumptuous entertainment, and I being one of the guests carefully observed every room and hall where the company were all seated, and was of the opinion that there must have been 1000 or more persons at table.

SHAW, JAMES 1805 *Scrivener.* Nelson's body was brought back from Trafalgar in a barrel of rum, and 30,000 mourners passed through the Painted Hall at Greenwich during the three day lying in state.

Mayor Shaw's barge headed the sombre procession upstream to St Paul's and weeping crowds lined both shores of the Thames to see the black-draped funeral barge carry their hero to his last berth. Except for the stormy skies and choppy water, prints of the event depict it as a stately Venetian procession in the style of Canaletto. When the coffin was being lifted ashore hundreds of sailors rushed forward to tear the flag off the bier and shred it into precious keepsakes.

SHORTER, JOHN 1687 *Goldsmith.* The Mayor seldom failed to open Bartholomew Fair at the beginning of August, but Shorter never completed the short ride from Guildhall to Smithfield. Accepting a tankard of mulled wine at Newgate he tilted it to drink, but as the heavy lid clattered to the cobbles his frightened horse reared and threw him.

By ancient custom a Lord Mayor dying in office can be buried in St Paul's. Cold comfort for Shorter's widow when he died next day.

SPENCER, JOHN 1594 *Clothworker.* Spencer was rich and mean, and locked his beautiful daughter in her room to thwart her noble but impoverished suitor. Bribing a servant to let her down from the window in a bread basket, she galloped away with her handsome knight on a white horse.

Spencer prospered by cornering vital commodities, and like Judde is one of the 'Ten Worthies' of St Helen's Bishopsgate. A skull and an hourglass, symbols of the futility of treasure on earth, mark the tomb of this miser who left nothing to the poor. Ironically, his daughter's descendant still enjoys the worldy title of Marquis of Northampton.

STAINES, WILLIAM 1800 *Carpenter.* Staines was a self-made man whose rough appearance and manners he never thought worthy of polishing. He had accumulated a fortune in the building trade, and married his cook along the way.

It may have been an implied insult to his wife's past slaving away over a hot stove, that made him shout at a guest toying with his food at a Guildhall banquet, "eat away, General, eat away, for we must pay all the same, eat or not eat".

STARLING, ROBERT 1669 *Brewer.* When the Great Fire threatened his property Alderman Starling, past Master of the Brewers and soon to be Lord Mayor, promised a fortune to anyone who would carry his possessions away from the flames creeping up Seething Lane. The danger past and his property safe he regretted the offer, and drove off the seamen waiting for their reward with a threat to have them prosecuted.

He had forgotten his neighbour in Seething Lane, and down it went for all time in Sam's diary: 'a very rich man, without children, the fire at next door to him in our lane, after our men had saved his house did give 2s 6d among thirty of them, and did quarrel with some that would remove the rubbish out of the way of this fire saying they came to steal'. Brewer's Hall was rebuilt after the Fire partly with a gift from Robert Starling, but his handsome £355 can never erase the memory of that niggardly half crown.

STOCKTON, JOHN 1470 *Mercer.* The Mayor made a small mark on history by taking to his bed at a critical moment in the Wars of the Roses.

The Yorkist Edward IV was firmly on the throne with the support of the City when the deposed Henry VI made a sudden unwelcome re- appearance in London. The threat was real, but unlikely to be permanent, so

Stockton feigned sickness and left his staunchly Lancastrian deputy to cope with the perilous situation. Henry was quickly captured and imprisoned in the Tower where he 'conveniently' expired, of multiple stab wounds to the chest. The Yorkists were back in the saddle until the fateful year of 1485.

STOKKER, WILLIAM 1485 *Draper*. Asking no awkward questions about the Princes in the Tower, the City accepted the firm rule of Richard III, Edward IV's brother, in 1483. Two years later it was even quicker to sense the Tudor wind blowing after the Battle of Bosworth, and all signs of the Yorkist White Rose had vanished before Henry VII rode into the capital.

After marrying Elizabeth of York, Henry invited the City worthies to a diplomatic reconciliation in Westminster Hall in May 1486. He knighted the Mayor and other citizens, and then entertained them with 'diverse subtleties and merriments' to a feast. Served by knights on bended knee the royal table had 60 dishes and the Mayor's 24, which took the aldermen until dawn to consume. They returned to the City all in favour of the Red Rose and Henry, who hated extravagance, must have felt his money well spent.

STRONG, THOMAS 1910 *Stationer*. A teetotal Lord Mayor, and toasted as such at his Mayoral Banquet.

He was a passionate advocate of 'Volapuk', a forgotten language of international of peace and brotherhood that was even less successful than its modern counterpart, Esperanto.

TRECOTHICK, BARLOW 1770 *Clothworker*. When the aged William Beckford died Trecothick took over as Lord Mayor, and then served a further full year.

He was the City MP and satirised by his opponents as 'Alderman Trick-a-Trick'. Influenced by his American mother he supported the rebellious Colonies and was damned as a traitor for being 'zealously attached, both by Nature and Education to Boston Principles and Bostonian Maxim; a strenuous Promoter of Faction and Disobedience to the Mother Country; and upon all

Occasions a fast Friend to the Interests of America, as opposed to those of Old England'.

Mayor Walworth many centuries before was accused of owning the Bankside stews, and slanderous tongues claimed that Trecothick's fortune came from ownership of similar bawdy houses in the City.

Trecothick like Beckford died in office, and he was succeeded by Wilkes' friend, Brass Crosby. For the next decade the City sent a stream of offensive and impertinent Remonstrances to Whitehall couched in flowery language which deceived no-one. Their warnings were clear about the 'fatal policy pursued towards the American colonies which can only alarm a free and commercial people'. The only thing to do was to take 'conciliatory measures as might restore union, confidence and peace ... if they would but listen the American colonies will remain with us, loyal and united'.

Arms of Sir William Treloar

TRELOAR, WILLIAM 1905 *Loriner*. He kept a diary of his great year. When presented to the Lord Chancellor he was offered 'red or white wine, spiced and warmed, and biscuits', but reckoned he had had to pay for them.

On the day of the Lord Mayor's Solemnity he appeared at Guildhall to find a meal 'ready for the aldermen, Sheriffs and others who were doomed to be in the show. A light breakfast it may be called, but I think a heavy luncheon would be the correct name for it. The procession made a start shortly after eleven, and I who came last, reached the Law Courts about 2 o'clock'.

Treloar was a Cornishman, and miners from the Truro School of Mining, children from the Ragged Schools and boys from the Shaftesbury Society were in his Procession. Lord Mayors were made of sterner stuff in his day and the Banquet, where traditionally the Prime Minister makes a major policy speech, was held the same evening. Now it takes place the following Monday.

Treloar represented the largest City ward, Farringdon Without to the west of St Paul's, and claimed he served the 'World, the Flesh and the Devil'. The World, the clamour of Fleet Street, the Flesh, the meat market of Smithfield and the Devil, the hordes of lawyers in the Temple.

He loved the young, and 800 refugee children were welcomed to Guildhall in 1914, and instead of a City dinner he also entertained the children of servicemen at the Front. He continued to organise the annual Christmas parties long after his Mayoral year with the help of the other London boroughs, and hampers were sent to the families of crippled children unable to get to the Mansion House. Donations from wellwishers swelled the Mayoral charity, and in 1920 the South Australian Sunbeam Society paid for the party.

The Lord Mayor Treloar College for disabled youngsters was founded in 1908 at Alton in Hampshire, and is now the largest boarding school for the physically handicapped with 285 pupils. Mayor Alan Traill appealed in 1984 for a Vocational Centre to teach the vital skills needed to earn a living once pupils leave the College, and this was so successful that future donations will go towards accommodation for more pupils.

VYNER, THOMAS 1653 *Goldsmith.* The puritans had the upper hand during the Commonwealth and had abolished the City Insignia and the church festivals of Christmas, Easter and Whitsun. Evelyn was scandalised to see Cromwell arrive in state in the City to dine with the Lord Mayor on Ash Wednesday, the solemn opening day of the Lenten Fast.

At the Restoration Vyner rushed to prove his loyalty to the City by presenting a new Mace, and to the King by setting up a statue at Stocks Market. It was actually of the King of Poland on horseback trampling the Turk, but by whipping off these two heads and substituting readymade ones of Charles II and Oliver Cromwell it served its purpose admirably. Not until the Mansion House was built on the site was this atrocity removed, and dumped on Vyner's descendants in Lincolnshire.

First flags of the American Colonists. The "rebels" had friends in the City of London

Miscellany of Mayors

W

WALWORTH – the 'trugging-house' keeper who killed Wat Tyler
WATERMAN – doubted Captain Blood had 'stolen' the Crown Jewels
WHITTINGTON – four times Lord Mayor, but never owned a cat
WILKES – the libertine who libelled his way to a free press
WOOD – self-important champion of an uncrowned Queen

Fishmongers

WAITHMAN, ROBERT 1823 *Framework Knitter.* Once the American Colonies won Independence, the City's kneejerk opposition to the government switched to the Napoleonic Wars. Many felt that a whiff of political and judicial revolution would not come amiss in England.

Waithman was a tireless promoter of electoral reform, and twin obelisks once stood in Ludgate Circus to him and John Wilkes, both aldermen of Farringdon Without. Waithman is hailed as 'a friend of Liberty in Evil Times', reference to the frustrating years leading up to the Reform Bill of 1832. His 'Times' obituary praised him for rising above his rivals as a 'steady and consistent advocate of the rights of his countrymen and the liberties and privileges of his fellow-citizens'.

The obelisk is now in Salisbury Square behind St Bride's, not far from where Waithman's draper's shop stood in Fleet Street.

WALDERNE, WILLIAM 1412/1422 *guild unknown.* Streams of Edicts and Ordinances poured from the Common Council to regulate trade in the City around the time of Agincourt. Most were resisted by the Companies who often resorted to naked bribery to tempt an official to turn a blind eye.

After an orgy of swan feasting in time of dearth the Brewers were forced by the Mayor to sell beer all the following week for a penny a gallon, instead of fourpence, and it rankled. After another breach of the rules, the Brewers bypassed the Mayor by giving two pipes of wine to his butler and two butts of wine to the Recorder. Wine they would have had to buy from the Vintners.

Mayor Walderne responded favourably to one petition after a boar and an ox were delivered to his door, but his successor William Crowmere was known to refuse all gifts.

WALLEIS, HENRY le 1273/1281 – 1283/1298 *Cordwainer.* On St Magnus Day 1298 the Mayor turned out with a thousand horsemen and all the Guilds to welcome home Edward I after the Battle of Falkirk, and the procession had the air of a Roman Triumph.

The Fishmongers stole the show with four gilded sturgeon carried on four horses, four silver salmons on four more horses followed by 46 knights riding in a formation that resembled the waves of the sea surrounding a figure of St Magnus of Orkney, whose church stands close to old Billingsgate Market.

WALWORTH, WILLIAM 1374/80 *Fishmonger* The Mayor struck first and asked questions afterwards when the Peasant's leader seized the King's bridle with threatening words. In Fishmongers Hall there is a statue in elm of Walworth brandishing the famous dagger, but it is *not* the one in the City Arms. The appearance of the short Roman sword of St Paul on the shield predates the Peasants' Revolt of 1381.

Brave Walworth, Knight, Lord Mayor, yet slew
Rebellious Tyler in his alarmes.
The King, therefore did give in lieu
The dagger in the City Arms

Landlords or patrons of brothels were never indictable, but the females who ran 'trugging houses' and the Joan Jollybodies who staffed them were always on the wrong side of the law and subject to harassment. A register of women of ill-fame was kept at Guildhall, and maybe not zealously updated for the purest of motives. Forbidden to reside within the Wall they congregated in the Bankside stews backing onto the Bishop of Winchester's Southwark palace, and were known as 'Winchester Geese'.

Many brothels were sacked and burned by the rebels causing considerable financial loss to the landlords, among them Mayor Walworth, so in protecting the King he may also have had his revenge on Tyler for spoiling his 'nice little earner'.

Two impressions of Walworth, Left, a contemporary picture-slaying Wat Tyler. Right, his statue in Fishmongers Hall.

WATERMAN, GEORGE 1671 *Skinner.* The Tower is outside the City, but when Captain Blood disguised as a clergymen got away with the Crown Jewels in December 1671 Mayor Waterman was called upon to hunt down any accomplices.

Blood was captured and imprisoned, but Charles II not only pardoned him for the double offence of attempted murder and armed robbery but welcomed him at court with a pension. Evelyn soon found himself dining with several French noblemen and the lionized Blood, who had a 'villainous unmerciful look, a false countenance but very well spoken and dangerously insinuating'. He privately voiced the amazement of many that such an impudent fellow should have escaped the block and hinted that the King had employed him for secret 'services which none alive could do so well as he'.

Captain Blood

Waterman may not have been too diligent in tracing any accomplices since rumour also hinted that Blood's royal employment might have extended to pawning the Crown Jewels abroad and sharing the proceeds with his debt-ridden monarch?

WATSON, BROOK 1796 *Musician.* London's only one-legged Lord Mayor. He had gone to sea as a youth and had a leg bitten off by a shark when swimming in Havana harbour. Opponents scorned his intellect although it did not prevent him becoming a governor of the Bank of England:

Modest Watson on his wooden leg.
Oh, had the monster, who for breakfast ate
That luckless limb, his nobler noddle met.
The best of workmen, nor the best of wood
Had scarce supplied him with a head so good'.

As a sailor Watson would have taken his responsibility as Admiral of the Port seriously and kept a close eye on Old Father Thames. Down river at Wapping was Execution dock where pirates were still despatched into the 19th century. The gallows were erected at low water mark and the victim's ordeal was prolonged by pinioning him as the tide was ebbing, and once dead he was left until three tides had washed over him.

These drownings, like the more frequent hangings at Newgate and Tyburn, were public entertainments and a pirate was expected to put on as good show as any highwayman.

One defiant pirate raised a cheer when he spotted a dockside whore among the crowd on Wapping Steps and swore that 'I have lain with that bitch three times and now she has come to see me hanged'.

WELLES, JOHN 1431 *Grocer.* Making play with his name for his Pageant, the Mayor had three wells flowing with wine in Cheapside dispensed by a trio of fair young virgins dressed as Mercy, Grace and Pity. Shading the wells were bare trees hung with almonds, dates, oranges and lemons all from the warehouses of this importer of fruit and nuts from as far away as Greece and Turkey.

The fate of a captured pirate

When trouble broke out in Norwich, one of England's major cities, Welles was appointed Warden in place of the deposed Mayor. Later he was sent as a trouble-shooter to the West Country, this time bearing a weapon rather than an olive branch:

John Welles, of London, Grocer, Mair,
Gave to Bristol this Sword Fair.

WHITTINGTON, RICHARD

1397/1397/1406/1419, *Mercer.* Nearly every-thing in the legend of Dick Whittington is false. He was never a penniless boy with a bundle on a stick seeking his fortune. Although he did come from Gloucestershire there was no reason for him turn back on Highgate Hill when Bow Bells rang out their lies about him being thrice Lord Mayor. Nor is there any record of a knighthood and, worst of all, not a word about a cat!

The pantomime Dick made his first appearance early 17th century, but the real man is worth remembering. He was the third son of Sir William Whittington of Pauntley a weathy merchant, and when he came to London he had a job waiting for him, possibly two. Some records say he started as a clerk at St John's Priory, Clerkenwell, but it is more likely he was bound apprentice by his father to a Mercer, John Fitzwarren.

Like any sensible and ambitious youth he eventually married his master's daughter, Alice. In time he became a Merchant Adventurer, an alderman and Master of the Mercers.

Coal kept the London fires burning, and Whittington may have taken coals from Newcastle. The coastal colliers were known as 'cats', and a trading ship of the Merchant Adventurers was called 'The Cat'. In any event, variations on the cat story appear in ancient Indian and Chinese legends.

In 1397 Mayor Adam Bamme died, so Sheriff Whittington took over and was then elected for the following year. He served again in 1406 and 1419 − making *four* times in all. He lent money to three English kings, and at a great banquet in Guildhall for Henry V and Katharine of Valois he threw the King's bond for £60,000 onto the fire 'to add something sweeter to the scent of cedar logs'. There is no record of a knighthood but it is unlikely the King would have failed to honour such a man.

In 1419 Whittington had built the largest public lavatory in London, a convenience in Vintry Ward with 60 seats each for Ladies and Gents, flushed with piped water. Modern regulations demand a ratio of one loo to fifteen staff so his was a relief to 1800 citizens, but this marvel was consumed in the Great Fire.

Richard and Alice had no children, and he left his great fortune for the benefit of the City he loved, and among his bequests was money to rebuild St Bartholomew's Hospital and Newgate Prison, manuscripts and desks to Christchurch library and almhouses for the poor and elderly. He is buried, 'lapped in lead', in St Michael Paternoster Royal, and a fine post-Blitz stained glass window shows young Dick with his faithful moggy. It goes to shows that you cannot kill off a good story, even though he left not so much as a groat to a cats' home!

WHYTE, THOMAS 1553 *Merchant Taylor*. Whyte was rated the richest man in London, and since he was only the second Merchant Taylor elected that century his Company was as proud as the Mayor and there was no stinting on the Show. Giants, savage green woodmen, trumpeters, singing waits, devils and St John the Baptist all mingled in his Triumph, and the following banquet was memorable. Merchant Taylor's Hall was the largest in the City and often used by other Mayors before the building of the Mansion House, and if Whyte returned today he would still find the worthy feasting in Threadneedle Street. Lady Jane Grey was tried in Guildhall, and on the warrant the

Whittington. Only later pictures showed him with a cat

name Whyte comes before Norfolk. As ever in the City the Mayor ranked higher than a Duke, even if he was the Earl Marshall of England.

WILKES, JOHN 1774 *Joiner*. 'Wilkes and Liberty' was the rallying cry of the London mob when their libertine champion stood for Brentford in the 1768 General Election, reckoned to be one of the most corrupt ever held. Liberty did not extend to Wilkes' opponents who were jostled and threatened by his supporters and even an ambassador's diplomatic immunity was ignored. The Austrian envoy was attacked, upended and had the magic number '45' painted on his boots.

Earlier Wilkes had libelled the King and the government in the 45th edition of his radical newspaper the 'North Briton'. A copy was burned by the common hangman at the Royal Exchange the cry of '45' was adopted as a political slogan and Wilkes was forced into exile. The printer of the 'North Briton', John Williams, was arrested and sentenced to stand in the pillory. This could be lethal with a hostile crowd, but the only danger to Williams was from the 10,000 admirers struggling to shake his hand. 'A gentleman produced a purse and made a collection for the benefit of the culprit' and when Williams was released he was presented with 200 guineas and carried off shoulder high to dinner.

Wilkes had returned from Paris for the Election fired with even more revolutionary ideas, and was elected by a huge majority on that riotous polling day. Parliament refused to let him take his seat, and only when he had been elected and rejected three more times, and won dubious 'respectability' as Lord Mayor, was he admitted to the Commons.

The American colonists had no more vocal supporter than Wilkes, and in years leading up to Independence he was an impassioned admirer of George Washington and Benjamin Franklin. He had as little respect for the church as he he had for the monarchy, having 'no Faith, but much Hope and Charity'.

Wilkes was a debauchee and a political opportunist, but he left two lasting achievements behind him. The right of the press to report Parliamentary debates, and the right of an elected MP to take his seat despite government attempts at exclusion.

John Wilkes

WILLIMOTT, ROBERT 1742 *Cooper*. Willimott refused to 'translate' to one of the Great Twelve as was customary. Once a Cooper, always a Cooper, and an inscribed silver salver commemorates his pride in his Company, and since then all Lord Mayors have had the option of remaining with their original Companies on election.

The London of George II was as dark and dangerous a place as it had been in Plantagenet times and the Mayor called for action against the 'confederacies of evil-disposed persons armed with bludgeons, pistols and cutlasses that infest lanes and private passages'. His plea was of no avail, there was no police force and the Watch had been a standing joke for centuries.

WOOD, MATTHEW 1815-16 *Fishmonger*. Wood had 'passed the chair' when he adopted the role of protector of the Queen in 1820, and the one-time apothecary and hop merchant revelled in his notoriety as champion of this wronged lady.

Married to the Prince Regent, soon to be George IV, blowsy, scandalous Caroline of Brunswick was an unlikely heroine, but her husband was so hated by the Londoners that they took her part. In a notorious trial he tried to divorce her for adultery, deprive her of her rights as Queen and forbid access to the Princess Charlotte, heir to the throne. Her acquittal was the signal for fantastic rejoicings, though few actually believed in her 'immaculate innocence', and her uncomprehending Italian major-domo's parrot cry of *non mi ricordo* 'I don't remember', in court was the catchphrase of the capital. Wood was in the forefront of the celebrations and happily paid for the hospitality dispensed from his town house by the Defendant.

The Company of Watermen serenaded Caroline from the river with a wind band and the firing of cannons, while the Founders constituted themselves the Queen's Guard with the slogan the 'Men of Metal'. The Lord Mayor, John Thorp, headed a deputation to congratulate the Queen on the triumph of justice in her favour, and it took twenty five carriages to transport all the red robed City functionaries to Wood's door.

In the end Wood's support did little to help Caroline's cause, and the new King George, though still bound to his detested wife in holy deadlock, took spectacular revenge by having Westminster Abbey locked against her at the coronation. The unhappy Caroline died soon afterwards, uncrowned, and by then unmourned by the fickle Londoners.

WOOTTON, NICHOLAS 1415 *Draper.* On the King's return from Agincourt, London Bridge was thronged with citizens, and Gog and Magog, to welcome him. Mayor Wootton and the Aldermen greeted 'Henry the Fifte, Kynge of England and of Fraunce, apparelled in scarlet with four hundred commoners well mounted and trimly horsed with rich collars and great chains. The clergy in solemn procession with rich crosses, sumptuous copes and massy censers received him

at St Thomas of Waterings'.

To their disappointment this 'grave and sober personage seemed little to regard the vain pomp and shows, insomuch that he would not suffer his helmet to be carried with him whereby the blows and dints upon it might have been seen by the people. Nor would he suffer any ditties to be made and sung by minstrels of his glorious victory because he would the praise and thanks should be altogether given to God'.

Henry cheered up enough to attend the Mayor's feast at Guildhall, and when the Dukes of Bedford, Gloucester and York objected to sitting below a mere commoner the King overruled his haughty relations. From that date the Mayor has ceded place to no-one but the Monarch in his own bailiwick.

WYFOLD, NICHOLAS 1450 *Grocer.* Jack Cade stormed in from Kent with his rabble of followers and briefly held the City at his mercy. Mayor Wyfold called on the citizens to defend their homes and the King's Majesty against the rebels. Cade rushed to Cannon Street and striking his sword against a famous stone, and in Shakespeare's words, proclaimed himself 'Lord of this City, and here sitting upon London Stone I command that, of the city's cost, the pissing-conduit run nothing but claret wine this first year of our reign'.

This went down a treat, and he had the mob in the hollow of his hand when he shouted 'there shall be in England seven halfpenny loaves sold for a penny and I will make it felony to drink small beer. All the realm shall be in common, there shall be no money and all shall eat and drink on my score'

His emotive, but impractical, egalitarian slogans echoed the cries of the Peasants Revolt seventy years earlier. The rebels swept on to Guildhall, held a mock trial of several grasping merchants, hustled them out into Cheapside and inexpertly beheaded them. But Wyfold soon had an armed force on the streets and the demoralised rebels were chased out of the City. Cade was caught and killed in Sussex, and his head soon joined those of his victims on London Bridge.

Jack Cade

LONDON STONE where Cade, during the Mayorality of Wyfold, proclaimed himself 'Lord of this City' is still there. Its origin is lost in myth, is it a druids' sacrificial altar or a Roman milestone, the marker from *Londinium* to distant Anglesey and Hadrian's Wall and Anglesey? Condemned as a traffic hazard in the 18th century, it was dug up and set behind an iron grille in St Swithin's. That blitzed church was not rebuilt and the Stone now has an improbable new home – set into the wall of the Bank of China. How many commuters pouring out of Cannon Street station spare it a glance, or link it with that first Mayor in 1189 who described himself as Henry Fitzailwyn 'goldsmith of London Stone'.

Livery Companies in Order of Precedence

1 **Mercers**
2 **Grocers**
3 **Drapers**
4 **Fishmongers**
5 **Goldsmiths**
6 **Skinners**
7 **Mecrhant Taylors**
8 **Haberdashers**
9 **Salters**
10 **Ironmongers**
11 **Vintners**
12 **Clothworkers**

13 Dyers
14 Brewers
15 Leathersellers
16 Pewterers
17 Barber-surgeons
18 Cutlers
19 Bakers
20 Wax-chandlers
21 Tallow chandlers
22 Armourers and Brasiers
23 Girdlers
24 Butchers
25 Saddlers
26 Carpenters
27 Cordwainers
28 Painter-stainers
29 Curriers
30 Masons
31 Plumbers
32 Innholders
33 Founders
34 Poulterers
35 Cooks
36 Coopers
37 Tylers and Bricklayers
38 Bowyers
39 Fletchers
40 Blacksmiths
41 Joiners and Ceilers
42 Weavers
43 Woolmen
44 Scriveners

45 Fruiterers
46 Plaisterers
47 Stationers and Newspaper Makers
48 Broderers
49 Upholders
50 Musicians
51 Turners
52 Basketmakers
53 Glaziers
54 Horners
55 Farriers
56 Paviors
57 Loriners
58 Apothecaries
59 Shipwrights
60 Spectacle Makers
61 Clockmakers
62 Glovers
63 Feltmakers
64 Framework Knitters
65 Needlemakers
66 Gardeners
67 Tin Plate Workers
68 Wheelrights
69 Distillers
70 Glass Sellers
71 Coachmakers and Coach Harness Makers
72 Gunmakers
73 Gold and Silver Wyre Drawers
74 Makers of Playing Cards
75 Fanmakers
76 Carmen
77 Master Mariners
78 Solicitors
79 Farmers
80 Air Pilots and Navigators
81 Tobacco Pipe Makers and Tobacco Blenders
82 Furniture Makers
83 Scientific Instrument Makers
84 Chartered Surveyors
85 Chartered Accountants
86 Chartered Secretaries
87 Builders Merchants

88 Launderers
89 Marketors
90 Actuaries
91 Insurers
92 Abitrators

93 Engineers
94 Fuellers
95 Lightmongers
96 Environmental Cleaners
97 Architects

Spot the Mayor

Second Saturday in November — Lord Mayor's Show, 10.30—13.30: London Wall, Guildhall, Princes Street, Bank, Cheapside, St Paul's, Ludgate Hill, Fleet Street and the Law Courts; 13.00—14.00: Embankment, Queen Victoria Street, Mansion House.

Wait in Chiswell Street just north of the Barbican around 16.00 to see coach and horses return to Whitbread's Brewery.

Other occasions to see the Lord Mayor, Sheriffs, Aldermen, Common Councilmen and Masters of more than 90 Livery Companies in ceremonial dress in Guildhall Yard include: 24 June — election of the Sheriffs, 10.00—13.00; 29 September — election of the Lord Mayor, 10.00—13.00; second Friday in November — admission of new Lord Mayor, 11.00—12.00.

The Lord Mayor carries out at least three or four engagements every weekday so the chances of seeing him are high.

If a Rolls Royce, 'LMO' (Lord Mayor's Office), is outside the Mansion House in Walbrook wait to see who comes out. There may be the bonus of the Sheriffs, aldermen or important guests.

Traditional events usually attended by the Lord Mayor include: second Tuesday in March – service in St Brides, Fleet Street, in memory of foundation of the Bridewell Royal Hospital; Friday before Good Friday — St Paul's, Annual Guild Service; first week in April – service in St Andrew Undershaft, St Mary Axe, in memory of the historian John Stow, and replacement of his quill pen; second Wednesday after Easter – Spital Sermon in St Lawrence Jewry; third week in May – service in St Olave Hart Street in memory of Samuel Pepys, with music of his time; June (date variable) — St Paul's, service for the Sons of the Clergy; 24 June – the Knollys Rose carried in procession from All Hallows by the Tower to the Mansion House (the ceremony dates from 1381); 21 September – St Matthew's Day Service of Christ's Hospital, the Blue Coat School, at St Sepulchre's Newgate, followed by the Marching Band in procession to the Mansion House.

Sites and Sightings in the City

City of London Information Centre
St Paul's Churchyard, EC4 8BX
Monday–Friday: 9.30–17.00
Saturday (Oct.–March): 10.00–12.30
Saturday: (April–Sept.): 10.00–16.00
Station: St Paul's
☎ (01) 606 3030

Guildhall
Gresham Street, EC2
Monday–Saturday: 10.00–17.00
Sunday (May–Sept. only): 14.30–
16.00)
Free; closed most bank holidays;
access ramp for wheelchairs
Stations: Bank, Moorgate, Mansion
House
☎ (01) 606 3030

Guildhall Library
Aldermanbury, EC2
Monday–Saturday: 9.30–17.00
Free use; no membership; no book
loans
☎ (01) 606 3030

Court of Common Council
Guildhall
Third Thursday in month: 13.00
Open to the public

Corporation of London Access Officer
Information for disabled
☎ (01) 606 3030, ext. 1995

Mansion House
Walbrook, EC4N 8BH
Group conducted tours by prior written
arrangement only; free
Station: Bank
☎ (01) 606 3030

Museum of London
London Wall, EC2
Tuesday–Saturday: 10.00–18.00
Sunday: 14.00–8.00
Closed Mondays
Permanent and special exhibitions
Free; facilities for disabled
Stations: Barbican, St Paul's
☎ (01) 600 3699

Bank of England Museum
Threadneedle Street, EC2
Entrance in Batholomew Lane
Winter: Monday–Friday: 10.00–18.00
Summer: Monday–Saturday: 10.00–
18.00
Sunday: 14.00–18.00
Free; braille leaflet and cassette,
disabled access difficult, phone in
advance
Station: Bank
☎ (01) 601 5793, ext. 5545

**London Tourist Board and Convention
Bureau**
26 Grosvenor Gardens, SWIW ODU
☎ (01) 730 3488
☎ (01) 730 4812 (riverboat
information)

Guild of Guide Lecturers
(Registered Blue Badge Guides)
2 Bridge Street, SWIA 2JR
☎ (01) 839 7438

St Paul's Cathedral
Sundays and weekdays
Services at stated times
Free, but donations appreciated
towards upkeep

City Churches
Area Dean's Office
Opening times vary; some mornings
 only
Parish churches have Sunday services
Many Monday–Friday only: lunchtime
 services, concerts, discussions
Free, but donations appreciated
 towards upkeep
☎ (01) 248 2705

City of London Flower Show
Guildhall, EC2
Two days early September

Whitbread Brewery Stables
Chiswell Street, EC1
By prior arrangement only
Disabled access admission charge
Stations: Old Street, Barbican
☎ (01) 606 4455

Barbican
Silk Street, EC2
Exterior podium and walkways:
 anytime
Foyer of Arts Centre: Monday–
 Sunday: according to performances
Free
Special exhibitions, fee charged
Facilities for disabled
Stations: Barbican, Moorgate
☎ (01) 638 4141

Lloyds of London
Lime Street, EC3
Monday–Friday: 10.00–14.30
Parties by arrangement: 14.30–15.45
☎ (01) 623 7100

Tower of London
Tower Hill, EC3
Monday–Saturday (March–Oct.):
 9.30–17.45
Sunday: 14.00–17.45
Closed Sunday in winter
Monday–Saturday (Nov.–Feb.): 9.30–
 16.30
Admission charge; limited facilities for
 disabled
Station: Tower Hill
☎ (01) 709 0765

Listen to the Band
Check for dates
Summer lunchtime concerts at:
St Paul's Steps; Paternoster Square
Tower Place; Finsbury Circus

Free newsletter 'Events in the City of
 London' available from Information
 Centre; 'City Recorder' and 'City
 Post' at newstands

*Note: it is advisable to check current
 admission times*

Lord Mayors of London in Alphabetical Order

Can you claim an ancestor in this unique list of Lord Mayors? Queen Elizabeth's England had a modest population of around two million, and since we all have two parents and four godparents these multiply to over four thousand relatives going back just to her reign, let alone to 1189. The odds on tracing a connection are not as long as you may think, and do not dismiss the idea because your name is spelt differently – spelling in the past was an 'optional extra'. Richard Whittington sometimes signs himself 'Whytyngdone', and Henry Keble, Kebyll Kybbil were all the same man.

Little is known of many of the Mayors in this list, but over 100 of those who did make their mark on London's history have found a place in the 'Miscellany'. Of course, once you have read about the exploits of some of them, the last thing you may want to do is claim any ancestral connection with such characters!

Name	Year	Name	Year	Name	Year
Abbot, Morris	1638	Bedingfield, Robert	1706	Bull, Frederick	1733
Abney, Thomas	1700	Bell, John	1907	Bungheye, Reginald de	1240
Abyndon, Stephen de	1315	Bellamy, Edward	1734	Burnell, John	1787
Acheley, Roger	1511	Bellinger, Robert	1966	Burnett, David	1912
Ackroyd, Cuthbert	1955	Benn, William	1746	Bury, Adam de†*	1364
Adams, Thomas	1645	Bennett, Thomas	1603	Calthorp, Martin	1588
Adrien, John	1270	Bère, Rupert de la	1952	Calvert, William	1748
Ailwyn Nicholas	1499	Bernes John†	1370	Cambell, James	1629
Alderman, James	1216	Besley, Robert	1869	Cambell, Thomas	1609
Alexander, Frank	1944	Bethwell, Slingsby	1755	Canynges, Thomas	1456
Aleyn, John*	1525	Betoyne, Richard de	1326	Capel, William*	1503
Allen, William (i)	1571	Billers, William	1733	Carden, Robert	1857
Allen, William (ii)	1867	Billesdon, Robert	1483	Carroll, George	1846
Alleyn, Thomas	1659	Billingsley, Henry	1596	Carter, John	1859
Allot, John	1590	Birch, Samuel	1814	Catworth, Thomas	1443
Alsop, Robert	1752	Blachford, John	1750	Cauntbrigge, William	1420
Amcotts, Henry	1548	Blades, George	1926	Cavendisshe, Stephen	1362
Anderson, John	1797	Blakiston, Mathew	1760	Challis, Thomas	1852
Andreu, James	1367	Blanke, Thomas	1582	Chalton, Thomas	1449
Andrews, Thomas*	1649	Bludworth, Thomas	1665	Champneys, John	1534
Ansley, John	1807	Blund, John le†	1301	Champyon, Richard	1565
Ascue, Christopher	1533	Boleyn, Geoffrey	1457	Chaplin, Francis	1677
Asgill Charles	1757	Bolles, Beorge	1617	Chapman, John	1688
Ashurst, William	1693	Bolton, William	1666	Chawry, Richard	1494
Ashwy, Ralph†	1241	Bonde, George	1587	Chester, William	1560
Askham, William	1403	Boteler, William	1515	Chichele, Robert*	1411
Astry, Ralhh	1493	Bowater, Frank	1938	Chichester John de	1369
Atkins, John	1818	Bowater, Ian	1969	Chigwell, Hamo de†*	1319
Atkyn, Thomas	1644	Bowater, Noel	1953	Child, Francis (i)	1698
Aubrey, Andrew†*	1339	Bowater, Thomas	1913	Child, Francis (ii)	1731
Avenon, Alexander	1569	Bower, Alfred	1924	Chitty, Thomas	1759
Aylmer, Lawrence	1508	Bowes, Martin	1545	Chiverton, Richard	1657
Aylwen, George	1948	Bowyer, William	1543	Clark, Richard	1784
Baddeley, John	1921	Boyce, Leslie	1951	Clarke, Edward	1696
Baldry, Thomas	1523	Boydell, John	1790	Clayton, Robert	1679
Bamme, Adam*	1390	Bradbury, Thomas	1509	Clitherow Christopher	1635
Barber, John	1732	Branche, John	1580	Clopton, Hugh	1491
Barentyn, Drogo*	1398	Brembre, Nicholas†*	1377	Clopton, Robert	1441
Barkham, Edward	1621	Breton, John le†*	1289	Cockayne, Francis	1750
Barnard John	1737	Bridgen, William	1763	Cokayne, William	1619
Barne, George (i)	1552	Bridges, George	1819	Colet, Henry*	1486
Barne, George (ii)	1586	Broadbridge, George	1936	Collett, Charles	1933
Barton, Henry*	1416	Brocas, Robert	1729	Collett, Christopher	1988
Basing, Adam de	1251	Brokle, John	1433	Combe, Harvey	1799
Basing, Solomon de	1217	Bromfield, Edward	1636	Conduit, Reginald de†	1334
Basset, Robert	1475	Broun, Stephen*	1438	Conyers, Gerard	1722
Bat, Gerard	1240	Brown, Anthony	1826	Cooke, Thomas	1462
Bat, Nicholas	1253	Browne, John	1480	Cooper, Edward	1919
Bateman, James	1716	Browne, Richard	1660	Copeland, William Taylor	1835
Bateman, Anthony	1663	Browne, William (i)	1507	Copynger, William	1512
Batho, Charles	1927	Browne, William (ii)	1513	Cork, Kenneth	1978
Bayley, William	1524	Brugge, John	1520	Cotes, John	1542
Baylis, Robert	1728	Bryce, Hugh	1485	Cotton, Allan	1625
Beachcroft, Robert	1711	Buckell, Cuthbert	1593	Cotton, William	1875
Becher, Edward	1727	Buckerel, Andrew†	1231	Coventre, John	1425
Beckford, William*	1762	Buckingham, Owen	1704	Cowan, John	1837

Wilkes, John	1774	Wire, David	1858	Wright, Edmund	1640
Wilkin, Walter	1895	Withers, William	1707	Wright, Thomas	1785
Wilkinson, George	1940	Wodecock, John	1405	Wroth, John	1360
Williams, John	1735	Wollaston, John	1643	Wyford, Nicholas	1450
Willimott, Robert	1742	Wontner, Hugh	1973	Wynger, John	1504
Wilson, Samuel	1838	Wood, Mathew†	1815	Yarford, James	1519
Winchester, Henry	1834	Woodroffe, Nicholas	1579	Yonge, John	1466
Winterbottom, Thomas	1751	Wotton, Nicholas*	1415	Zuche, Alan la	1267

Note: There have been less than 800 Mayors in the past eight centuries because in the early years Mayors marked * served more than once and/or others marked † held office for several years.

Titles in the London Pride Collection.

Future titles

From leading booksellers or direct from the publishers please allow 45p postage and packing.

Australian London by Kate Murphy.

Discover the links between the old Colonial Capital and the World's largest inhabited island. Indispensible to Australians visiting London and Londoners with an interest in Australia.
Amusing illustrations by an Australian Artist. 80 pages. £2.95

Wheels of London by Deborah Friend.

From donkey cart to tube train. The fascinating story of the first city to face the problems of urban transport. Compelling reading for transport buffs, commuters and environmentalists.
Photo illustrations 96 pages £3.95

Bus Top London by Brian Murphy.

Modern shopfronts and office entrances hide the London that exists above street level. This book takes you on a series of bus top trips to see the London hardly anyone knows.
Photo illustrations 96 pages £3.95

The Cockney Cook Book by Brian Murphy

Authentic cockney recipes spiced with insights into the lives of history's first streetwise people.
With wonderful whimsical drawings 80 pages. £2.95

Cabbie! by Sir Lou and Barrie Sherman.

A cabbie, who was knighted for public service, records over half a century of cabbie wit and wisdom. Packed with the excitement and pathos that is the life of the London taxi driver. Once you have read it a ride in a taxi will never be the same again.
Illustrated 96 pages £3.95

Certainly not in the London Pride Collection!

Forty ways to ruin a party by Brian Murphy.

A cynical view that parties are only thrown to enhance the hosts standing. In a competitive world where to win is all that matters this book tells you how to ensure your own party looks good by ruining the other persons.
Introducing a brilliant new Welsh cartoonist.
48 pages £1.95